Culturally Responsive Teaching and The Brain

This book is dedicated to my children,
Morgan and Zindzi.
You have been my greatest teachers.

Culturally Responsive Teaching and The Brain

Promoting Authentic Engagement and Rigor
Among Culturally and
Linguistically Diverse Students

Zaretta Hammond

Foreword by Yvette Jackson

CORWIN
A SAGE Company

FOR INFORMATION:

Corwin

A SAGE Company

2455 Teller Road

Thousand Oaks, California 91320

(800) 233-9936

www.corwin.com

SAGE Publications Ltd.

1 Oliver's Yard

55 City Road

London EC1Y 1SP

United Kingdom

SAGE Publications India Pvt. Ltd.

B 1/I 1 Mohan Cooperative Industrial Area

Mathura Road, New Delhi 110 044

India

SAGE Publications Asia-Pacific Pte. Ltd.

3 Church Street

#10-04 Samsung Hub

Singapore 049483

Printed in the United States of America.

ISBN 978-1-4833-0801-2

Acquisitions Editor: Dan Alpert

Associate Editor: Kimberly Greenberg

Editorial Assistant: Cesar Reyes

Production Editor: Amy Schroller

Copy Editor: Kimberly Hill

Typesetter: C&M Digitals (P) Ltd.

Proofreaders: Laura Webb and Victoria Reed-Castro

Indexer: Karen Wiley

Cover Designer: Anupama Krishnan

Marketing Manager: Stephanie Trkay

This book is printed on acid-free paper.

SUSTAINABLE FORESTRY INITIATIVE

Certified Chain of Custody
At Least 10% Certified Forest Content
www.sfiprogram.org
SFI-01028

21 22 23 24 25 36 35 34 33

Contents

Foreword

Neuroscience research has substantiated a reality that we should relish: We are all wired for expansive learning, high intellectual performances, and self-determination!

Although this has been verified, there is a syllogism for educators that should be proven to be true and yet has still not become the performance standard: If all brains are wired for expansive learning, high intellectual performances, and self-determination, then students of color should be experiencing this state of being. Since neuroscience has proven the validity of the premise of this syllogism, this is the time for a seminal question to be reckoned with: Why are so many students of color underachieving?

We can't overstate the fact that this reality is a complex conundrum, requiring the need to consider and address a myriad of underregarded factors, the most prevalent being lack of belief in the innate intellectual potential of these students. The most poignant consideration to address in order to answer this seminal question takes us back to the finding from neuroscience: If all students are wired for expansive learning and self-determination, what is needed to activate that wiring for optimal connectivity for students of color? The answer: mediating learning through cultural responsive teaching.

When the brain encounters information, especially during the act of reading and learning, it's searching for and making connections to what is personally relevant and meaningful. What is relevant and meaningful to an individual is based on his or her cultural frame of reference. Finding cultural relevance and personal connections give us perspective, engages our attention, and assists us in interpreting and inferring meaning, enabling the depth of understanding and interest needed for what are considered acts of high intellectual processing such as conceptualizing, reasoning, or theorizing (Jackson, 2011).

Unfortunately, teachers are too often unaware of the fact that the connections they choose to assist students in understanding concepts being taught are in fact "cultural," reflective of the lived, familiar experiences of students who are not students of color, leaving students of color in a state of disconnect, and often a deep sense of frustration. As much as they search to find the relevance that would enable them to be engaged and make meaning, they are unable, so their innate ability for high levels of cognitive processing is inhibited.

Cultural relevance is the key to enabling the cognitive processing necessary for learning and imperative for engaging and unleashing intellectual potential for students of color. Neuroscience has informed us that it is the catalyst that activates the wiring for neural connectivity to be optimized for learning. But why? And how can we use this information to assist the tens of thousands of teachers around the country who search tirelessly for what's needed to design their teaching to be culturally responsive to students of color so they can perform at the high levels they believe these students are capable of attaining?

Cultural responsiveness is not a practice; it's what informs our practice so we can make better teaching choices for eliciting, engaging, motivating, supporting, and expanding the intellectual capacity of ALL our students. *Culturally Responsive Teaching and The Brain: Promoting Authentic Engagement and Rigor* elucidates for us the neuroscience behind why culture is the fundamental imperative for learning. Zaretta Hammond translates this science into a framework that enables teachers to both create the relationships *and* apply strategies that foster culturally responsive teaching to optimize learning, enabling us to make real the implication of the syllogism that students of color can demonstrate the expansive learning, high intellectual performances, and self-determination for which their brains are wired to achieve.

Dr. Yvette Jackson

Acknowledgments

I remember the day in 2000 a principal suggested I write this book as she left my conference breakout session. I had just presented findings from my 3-year pilot program on educational equity as part of the Bay Area School Reform Collaborative (BASRC) annual conference. I thought it was ironic for her to say that given so very few people had attended this session where I talked about equity, instruction, and brain science. But the idea was planted. Over the years, I found other teachers, leaders, and researchers interested in the topic. Every conversation and article shared has contributed to this book. I thank each one of you for being part of my personal learning community. I also want to thank those teachers who invited me into their classrooms to explore these ideas in real time and shared their practice with me.

I also want to appreciate my National Equity Project family. My two tours of duty allowed space to practice and refine many of these ideas. To LaShawn Route-Chatmon, I appreciate your continuous encouragement. Victor Cary, I am so glad you liked talking about neuroscience just as much as I did. And a special thank you to coaches, Mark Salinas and Colm Davis, who were so kind to read the first draft and offer insightful feedback. It's a better book because of you.

For their commitment to ensuring the next generation of teachers are culturally conscious, I'd like to acknowledge my St. Mary's College colleagues, Clifford Lee and Rania Leon. I am privileged to teach with you.

A shout out to Steve Jubb, Michelle Grant-Groves, Sarah Breed, Mica Mosely, Shane Safir, Leslie Plettner, and Susan Sandler. You all have been my cheerleaders over the years. A special thanks to Professor Nikole Richardson at Mills College who reminded me that I wasn't writing for myself but for teachers who were committed to being culturally responsive educators.

Becki Cohn-Vargas, you deserve a special thanks for being a great matchmaker and introducing me to Dan. I so appreciated our shoptalk over lunch. Thanks to my editor, Dan Alpert, for being a champion for this book during a very difficult personal period. My appreciations also go out to Kimberly Greenberg and Cesar Reyes for their help in getting all the pieces of the book in the right places.

There are no words to express my gratitude to my family for enduring the disruptions of daily life so I could write this book. Your encouragement has been my oxygen. Last but not least, I want to thank William, my spouse and partner in life. Thirty years ago when we formed our partnership you promised I'd never have to sacrifice my own identity and dreams. This book is living proof of that promise. Thank you.

PUBLISHER'S ACKNOWLEDGMENTS

Corwin gratefully acknowledges the contributions of the following reviewers:

Marsha Basanda
Fifth Grade Teacher
Greenville County Schools, Monarch Elementary
Simpsonville, SC

Charla Bunker
Literacy Specialist
Great Falls Public Schools
Great Falls, MT

Marcia Carlson
Sixth Grade Teacher
Crestview Elementary School
Clive, IA

Becki Cohn-Vargas
Director, Not In Our School
The Working Group
Oakland, CA

Jennifer Craft
Staff Development Teacher
Montgomery Blair High School
Silver Spring, MD

Rick DuVall
Executive Director
Central Florida Education Consortium
Orlando, FL

About the Author

 **Zaretta Hammond** is a former classroom English teacher who has been doing instructional design, school coaching, and professional development around the issues of equity, literacy, and culturally responsive teaching for the past 18 years. She teaches as a lecturer at St. Mary's College's Kalmanovitz School of Education in Moraga, California.

In addition to consulting and professional development, she has been on staff at national education reform organizations, including the National Equity Project and the former Bay Area School Reform Collaborative (BASRC). She has trained instructional coaches in reading development, especially targeted at students of color and English learners. She has also designed national seminars such as the 3-day *Teaching with a Cultural Eye* series for teachers and school leaders. She is regularly invited to present at regional and national conferences. She has authored articles that have appeared in publications such as *Phi Delta Kappan*.

Along with a focus on culturally responsive teaching, Ms. Hammond has a strong research agenda around literacy, vocabulary development, and equity. She has designed culturally responsive tutor training programs aimed at volunteer reading tutors for a variety of nonprofit organizations. She is currently designing a literacy program to accelerate low reading skills among high school students. She holds a Master's in Secondary English Education.

She also writes the popular ready4rigor.com blog. Zaretta is the proud parent of two young adult children, both of whom she taught to read before they went to school. She resides in Berkeley, California, with her husband and family. Contact Zaretta Hammond at zlhammond@ready4rigor.com

Introduction

Believe it or not, the seeds of this book were planted in me way back in Miss Alexander's first grade class at Lafayette Elementary School in San Francisco. The school was located in the Richmond district in the city, a community made up mostly of middle class White families, first- and second-generation Japanese and Russian immigrant families. I was one of about a dozen African American children in a student population of just over 200 students, including my brother and sister. My family alone made up a third of the Black students in the school. I always felt I didn't belong there, figuratively and literally.

In reality, I lived on the other side of town in public housing known as "the pink projects" in the predominantly Black Hunter's Point community. My mother, a single teen parent who had three children by the time she was 22 years old, knew that the only way out of the projects for us was through education. When it was time for us to go to school, she visited the neighborhood school in Hunter's Point and found run-down facilities and low expectations for the children. So, she took matters into her own hands. She used her parents' address to enroll us in Lafayette Elementary across town. My grandparents, both hardworking but illiterate, had come to California at the tail end of the Great Black Migration in 1940. The Great Migration was the movement of two million African Americans out of the rural South to urban states in the Northeast, Midwest, and West between 1919 and 1940 to escape the oppression of Jim Crow in the South and take advantage of economic opportunities up North. My grandfather worked as a longshoreman at the Port of Oakland and my grandmother worked as a maid cleaning houses for upper class White families in Pacific Heights and Nob Hill in San Francisco. They bought their home in the Richmond neighborhood 1 year before I was born. They were the first and only Black family on the block for over 20 years.

Every day, we took the hour-long ride on public transportation to school by ourselves. Mom had to go to work. Our daily trip included getting up early to take one bus out of Hunter's Point and transferring to another in order to get to school on time, with my brother, a third grader, in charge of me and my sister, a kindergartener. The principal and teachers turned a blind eye to the fact that we lived outside the attendance zone for Lafayette as long as we "behaved" ourselves. (I would test that implicit agreement many times before graduating in the sixth grade.)

Back home on the playground in the projects, it slowly became clear to me that my brother, sister, and I were getting a different kind of education at Lafayette than the kids in the projects who went to the local school. I have vivid memories of cuddling up one-on-one with Miss Alexander in the reading corner as I read to her. By second grade, I had learned to read well and fell in love with books while the neighborhood kids were struggling with reading. In the fourth grade with Miss Martini, we were doing project-based learning before it was even called project-based learning. On the other hand, back in the neighborhood, my playmates were doing fill-in-the-blank worksheets. At Lafayette, we had Model United Nations in fifth and sixth grade where we learned history, geography, economics, and social studies in integrated ways.

When I was in the fifth grade, Lafayette Elementary School was integrated. It was one of the first 12 schools in San Francisco to integrate under a court-ordered desegregation decree. By this time, my family and I had moved from the projects in Hunter's Point to public housing in the Fillmore/Western Addition neighborhood in San Francisco. All of a sudden at Lafayette, there were other students of color from my neighborhood. But I noticed a big difference in the classroom. They struggled with analytical tasks and many were in remedial reading groups. The difference I came to realize was I had been taught to use my mind well, process information effectively, and do analytical reading. From the first grade, students at Lafayette Elementary were being prepared to take on increasingly more rigorous content as we moved toward sixth grade. We were taught to be independent, self-directed learners. That was not the case for the new kids that showed up. I was witnessing the achievement gap firsthand. Despite coming to a school that had high quality teachers and instruction, the gaps in their knowledge and skill by fifth grade were too great for them to be independent learners without intense focus and support.

After many decades of attention, the achievement gaps I witnessed as an elementary school student are still with us. The things I witnessed and experienced as a student of color then aren't significantly different from what many students of color experience in schools today. Despite 30 plus years of education reform, the words of education researcher, Charles Payne, are truer than ever: There's been "so much reform and so little change" (2008).

Many educators have been looking to culturally responsive teaching as a way to close our achievement gaps given the intense focus on rigor in the classroom with the arrival of the Common Core State Standards. But for some, culturally responsive teaching (CRT) is simply an engagement strategy designed to motivate racially and culturally diverse students. It seems simplistic to think that students who feel marginalized, academically abandoned, or invisible in the classroom would reengage simply because we mention tribal kings of Africa or Aztec empires of Mexico in the curriculum or use "call and response" chants to get students pumped up. For some, it is seen as a "bag of tricks" with magical properties that don't allow us to really know how it works. Because it seems so mysterious, many teachers don't bring the same rigor, consistency, and serious implementation to it as they do with other instructional practices.

More than a motivational tool, culturally responsive teaching is a serious and powerful tool for accelerating student learning. The more we learn from neuroscience, the clearer it becomes as to why and how it works. That's what this book is about: the connection between brain-based learning and rigorous culturally responsive teaching. Based on my 18 years as an educator and student of neuroscience, I believe culturally responsive teaching has the power to close achievement gaps. When practiced correctly and consistently, it can get underperforming students of color who are caught on the wrong side of the achievement gap ready for rigorous learning by building their brainpower. Dr. Edmund Gordon and his colleagues with the National Study Group for the Affirmative Development of Academic Ability housed at Teachers College at Columbia University, in their 2004 task force report, "All Students Reaching the Top," highlighted what a growing body of research around closing the achievement gap has found: Building brain power is the missing link to closing the achievement gap for underperforming culturally and linguistically diverse students.

THE MARRIAGE OF NEUROSCIENCE AND CULTURALLY RESPONSIVE TEACHING

Every year, neuroscientists learn more and more about how the brain learns. For instance, we are learning about the importance of the brain's executive functions in directing learning, problem solving, and self-regulation. Honestly, I wish I had this information when I was in my teacher education program. Any references to the brain and learning were limited to my one semester of Ed Psych. Instead, we spent most of our time learning about the learning theories of Piaget, Skinner, and Thorndike but not their application to everyday teaching. We talked about stages of development but never actually talked in detail about the brain as a natural learning apparatus. During my time as a preservice teacher, we spent even less time talking about culturally responsive teaching, although we touched on educational equity and the achievement gap briefly.

Brain-based learning strategies from neuroscience and culturally responsive teaching have always been presented as two separate, unrelated branches of educational practice. Yet teacher educators Geneva Gay and Gloria Ladson-Billings each describe culturally responsive pedagogy as encompassing the social-emotional, relational, and cognitive aspects of teaching culturally and linguistically diverse students. Cognition and higher order thinking have always been at the center of culturally responsive teaching, which makes it a natural partner for neuroscience in the classroom. This book sets out to explicitly highlight the natural intersection between so-called "brain-based learning" and culturally responsive teaching. I believe one of the biggest benefits of looking at these two approaches together is that we can better recognize what impact certain culturally responsive practices have on student learning. Neuroscience also offers a way to understand and organize our culturally responsive teaching practice.

MAKING CULTURALLY RESPONSIVE TEACHING ACCESSIBLE

The question I hear from many teachers is: *How can we make culturally responsive teaching more accessible as a practice?* The first step in learning to use culturally responsive practices is understanding what those practices are and how they fit into our understanding of cognitive science.

Because there's so much confusion over what culturally responsive teaching is and how it works, I started assembling strategies from culturally responsive pedagogy, brain-based learning, and equity and braiding them together into a framework that made it easier to understand and apply in the classroom. I began testing parts of it in the programs I designed as a curriculum developer and facilitated as a professional developer. The first opportunity came as the director of The Equity Initiative at the Bay Area School Reform Collaborative (BASRC), an Annenberg-funded school reform initiative, and then as an independent reading tutor trainer with Community Solutions Network. As part of a team of talented coaches who designed an inquiry-based approach to instructional coaching, I was able to bring some of these approaches and frames to the Partnership for Learning program at the National Equity Project and apply them to instructional coaching. As the chief designer of the professional development seminar, Teaching with a Cultural Eye, I got another chance to refine the frame and share it with teachers and school leaders.

I offer it here as a way to help educators understand how to operationalize culturally responsive teaching, especially in service of our most vulnerable and underserved students.

MY INTENTION OF THIS BOOK

Language is powerful. When you are able to name a thing, it moves out of the realm of mystery into concreteness. For too long, culturally responsive teaching has been relegated to this realm of magic and mystery, knowledge that only a select few possess. When we are able to recognize and name a student's learning moves and not mistake culturally different ways of learning and making meaning for intellectual deficits, we are better able to match those moves with a powerful teaching response. My intention in this book is to expand teachers' vocabulary for talking about culturally responsive teaching, especially for underperforming culturally and linguistically diverse students. For too long, the conversation has been dominated by the idea of the "culture of poverty" as an organizing social and intellectual frame for teaching marginalized culturally and linguistically diverse students. In these pages, I offer new concepts and frames for thinking about culturally responsive teaching as an extension of brain-based learning. Turning concepts into practices takes focus, feedback, and reflection. My hope is that soon this book in your hands will be highlighted, underlined, and dog-eared as you use it to build your background knowledge and culturally responsive toolkit. May it lead you into many rich conversations with your colleagues about leveraging the natural learning systems of culturally diverse students in our ongoing efforts to close the achievement gap.

WHAT THIS BOOK IS AND WHAT IT ISN'T

This book isn't a how-to guide on developing culturally responsive lesson plans in every subject area. The Ready for Rigor frame is not a prescriptive program outlining how to do culturally responsive teaching. Instead, I want you to think of culturally responsive teaching as a mindset, a way of thinking about and organizing instruction to allow for great flexibility in teaching. The Ready for Rigor frame simply attempts to organize the principles and tools that should be staples in the toolkit of every culturally responsive teacher. It focuses on helping teachers understand the brain-based principles that govern culturally responsive teaching so that we can stimulate underperforming students' cognitive development and grow self-directed learners. Too few education researchers, with the exception of Edmund Gordon, Yvette Jackson, Carol Lee, Augusta Mann, A. Wade Boykins, Rosa Hernandez-Sheets, Aida Walqui, Pedro Noguera, and the late Asa Hilliard, have explicitly focused on building underserved students' cognitive resources as a strategy to closing the achievement gap. Boykin and Noguera (2011) said it best, "when such assets are not yet part of a student's repertoire, educators must directly provide for their acquisition and use" (p. 114). The Ready for Rigor frame attempts to provide some insight into how we can help students acquire and use their natural, culturally grounded cognitive resources. In addition, it illuminates the connection between culture, schooling, and the larger dynamics of race, class, and language in society that shape the educational experiences and outcomes of many students of color and English learners.

NAMING OUR STUDENTS: A NOTE ABOUT TERMINOLOGY

Traditionally, in education we talk about the achievement gap in terms of Black and White—African American students and White students. Since the influx of immigrant families over the past few decades, we have started to include Latino students in the group of students negatively impacted by the achievement gap, many of whom are English learners. In this book, I often name African American and Latino students when talking about cultural responsiveness in the classroom. Please note that I use African American and Latino students as proxies for the larger group of diverse students of color in our classrooms, especially those groups that have traditionally been unacknowledged, such as Pacific Islander and First Nation students. It is important that we also include in our definition students of South Asian and Asian descent when talking about the achievement gap. Too often, we identify these two groups as high achievers who don't need culturally responsive teaching. In reality, we have many students from Hmong, Vietnamese, and Cambodian backgrounds who are struggling to be heard and supported in school.

You will see that I use the terms *students of color* and *culturally and linguistically diverse students* interchangeably throughout the book. I want you to keep in mind that English learners are always included when I refer to students of color, even though there are unique issues around language that all educators need to be familiar with and address specifically.

TEACHER EXAMPLES

I have tried to provide some short anecdotes of teachers' attempts to change their practice to incorporate the approaches outlined in the book in their teaching practice. They are composites of the teachers who have invited me into their classrooms in past years. I have changed their names and identifying characteristics.

WHO IS THE BOOK FOR?

I write this book for three main audiences:

Classroom teachers. Most teachers across the country have gone through workshops and seminars on culturally responsive pedagogy, equity, or brain-based learning. This book provides teachers with an understanding of how all three are related and interdependent along with practical strategies for turning new conceptual understanding into on-the-ground teaching practices. It is designed to support teachers' continued growth and development as culturally responsive educators. It's written so an individual teacher can use it to build her teaching practice or it can be used as a study guide within a professional learning community.

Instructional coaches. More and more school districts are supporting teacher development with ongoing instructional coaching. This book is also for instructional coaches who are charged with supporting teachers around culturally responsive teaching. Instructional coaches when they come with an equity lens set up "creative tension" between the teacher's vision of a culturally supportive classroom and current reality. When armed with the right tools and information, they act as "instructional sherpas," guiding a teacher on his own professional capacity building journey. Hopefully, this book will provide coaches with some new language for talking about culturally responsive teaching that focuses on cognitive development rather than on simple engagement strategies.

Instructional leaders. Principals and teacher-leaders play a critical role in creating a school culture that allows for the care and nurturing of culturally responsive learning practices and spaces, both for students and teachers. This book hopefully will provide a conceptual frame that informs and supports their instructional leadership.

OUTLINE OF THE BOOK

Ready for Rigor is an interdisciplinary approach to understanding cultur-ally responsive teaching. It approaches culturally responsive teaching as an adaptive endeavor rather than a technical fix, which means that the quality of relationships between teacher and students are just as impor-tant as the technical strategies used to get students to perform at higher levels. The book is divided into three parts. In Part I, we focus on the first area of the Ready for Rigor frame, Awareness. In Chapter 1, we look at the promise of culturally responsive teaching in supporting our most vulner-able students. I explain the relationship between helping students of color who are dependent learners and culturally responsive teaching. We also look at the role neuroscience can play in helping us understand how to implement it more successfully. In this chapter, I introduce the Ready for Rigor framework that helps organize culturally responsive teaching and guides us through the other chapters in the book. Chapter 2 looks at the role culture plays in culturally responsive teaching and offers a unique way to think about it. Chapter 3 reviews the connection between culture, brain structures, and building brainpower. In Chapter 4, we return to looking at personal "inside-out" work culturally responsive teachers must do to prepare themselves to be effective. Part II focuses on Learning Part-nerships and covers Chapters 5 through 7. Chapter 5 outlines the founda-tional role effective student-teacher relationships play in culturally respon-sive teaching. Chapter 6 explores the special stance and skills teachers need in order to leverage relationships and culture to help dependent learners cultivate the right mindset as they move toward independence. In Chapter 7, we look at the strategies that build academic mindset in cultur-ally congruent ways. Part III focuses on Building Intellective Capacity and covers Chapters 8 through 9. Chapter 8 focuses on information processing and building students' intellective capacity through cognitive routines. Chapter 9 looks at the importance of creating a socially and intellectually safe classroom community that encourages students to take more cogni-tive risks. Finally, in the Epilogue, we think together about how we lead for equity outside the classroom as culturally responsive educators. Each chapter ends with these common parts:

- **Chapter Summary**—a set of big ideas from the chapter
- **Invitation to Inquiry**—a set of questions for reflection and fur-ther investigation
- **Going Deeper**—a set of resources for learning more and building background knowledge

SUGGESTIONS FOR GETTING
THE MOST OUT OF THE BOOK

- ***Read with intention and purpose***. Ask yourself a guiding question as you read: *How do I want to grow as a culturally responsive educator? What do I want to know more about or what questions or concerns do I have?*
- ***Read the book with a highlighter and a notebook.*** As you read, mine the content for the nuggets of information and insight that resonate with you. Pull out those that build on what you already know. Make explicit connections to schoolwide or professional learning community (PLC) initiatives or other approaches for improving outcomes for low performing students. Summarize in your own words so that you help your brain assimilate the new information.
- ***Customize tools and strategies***. Think through how you might tailor strategies and tools to fit your grade level, school context, or your own personality and style.
- ***Take bite-sized action***. Begin with one or two strategies for building relationships and one or two for building intellective capacity. If you are just beginning to explore culturally responsive teaching, don't allow yourself to get overwhelmed by believing you have to do it all. If you are a veteran of CRT, focus on one or two areas you'd like to strengthen in your practice.
- ***Practice action research***. Based on your guiding question, observe your current practice or student learning behaviors to establish a baseline. Put your bite-sized actions in motion. Collect data regularly. Create space and time to analyze and interpret it against the Ready for Rigor frame. Then reflect and adjust your practices.
- ***Invite others to join you on the journey***. Form an inquiry group or book circle as a way to foster collaboration and accountability around your action research.

PART I

Building Awareness and Knowledge

1 Climbing Out of the Gap

Supporting Dependent Learners to Become Independent Thinkers

Education either functions as an instrument which is used to facilitate integration of the younger generation into the logic of the present system and bring about conformity or it becomes the practice of freedom, the means by which men and women deal critically and creatively with reality and discover how to participate in the transformation of their world.

—Paulo Freire, *Pedagogy of the Oppressed*

The chronic achievement gap in most American schools has created an epidemic of dependent learners unprepared to do the higher order thinking, creative problem solving, and analytical reading and writing called for in the new Common Core State Standards. One of the goals of education is not simply to fill students with facts and information but to help them learn how to learn. Classroom studies document the fact that underserved English learners, poor students, and students of color routinely receive less instruction in higher order skills development than other students (Allington & McGill-Franzen, 1989; Darling-Hammond, 2001; Oakes, 2005). Their curriculum is less challenging and more repetitive. Their instruction is more focused on skills low on Bloom's taxonomy. This type of instruction denies students the opportunity to engage in what neuroscientists call **productive struggle** that actually grows our brainpower (Means & Knapp, 1991; Ritchhart, 2002). As a result, a disproportionate number of culturally and linguistically diverse students are dependent learners.

Here is the problem. On his own, a dependent learner is not able to do complex, school-oriented learning tasks such as synthesizing and analyzing informational text without continuous support. Let's not misunderstand the point—dependent doesn't mean deficit. As children enter school, we expect that they are dependent learners. One of our key jobs in the early school years is to help students become independent learners. We expect students to be well on their way to becoming independent learners by third grade, but we still find a good number of students who struggle with rigorous content well into high school, mostly students of color.

The closest we usually come to talking about this situation is the popular "Read by Third Grade" campaigns. We say children are *learning to read* up until third grade then shift to *reading to learn.* The same is true with cognition. In the early grades, we teach children habits of mind and help them build cognitive processes and structures so that as they move through school they are able to do complex thinking and independent learning.

For culturally and linguistically diverse students, their opportunities to develop habits of mind and cognitive capacities are limited or non-existent because of educational inequity. The result is their cognitive growth is stunted, leaving them dependent learners, unable to work to their full potential. In the *New Jim Crow: Mass Incarceration in the Age of Colorblindness,* Michelle Alexander (2012) suggests that this dependency is the first leg of the "school-to-prison pipeline" for many students of color. According to the Southern Poverty Law Center, the school-to-prison pipeline is a set of seemingly unconnected school policies and teacher instructional decisions that over time result in students of color not receiving adequate literacy and content instruction while being disproportionately disciplined for non-specific, subjective offenses such as "defiance." Students of color, especially African American and Latino boys, end up spending valuable instructional time in the office rather than in the classroom. Consequently, they fall further and further behind in reading achievement just as reading is becoming the primary tool they will need for taking in new content. Student frustration and shame at being labeled "a slow reader" and having low comprehension lead to more off-task behavior, which the teacher responds to by sending the student out of the classroom. Over time, many students of color are pushed out of school because they cannot keep up academically because of poor reading skills and a lack of social-emotional support to deal with their increasing frustration.

Figure 1.1 Dependent Learner Characteristics vs. Independent Learner

Many culturally and linguistically diverse students are "dependent learners" who don't get adequate support to facilitate their cognitive growth. Consequently, they are not able to activate their own neuroplasticity.

The Dependent Learner	The Independent Learner
• Is dependent on the teacher to carry most of the cognitive load of a task always • Is unsure of how to tackle a new task • Cannot complete a task without scaffolds • Will sit passively and wait if stuck until teacher intervenes • Doesn't retain information well or "doesn't get it"	• Relies on the teacher to carry some of the cognitive load temporarily • Utilizes strategies and processes for tackling a new task • Regularly attempts new tasks without scaffolds • Has cognitive strategies for getting unstuck • Has learned how to retrieve information from long-term memory

In recent years, there's been a lot of talk about the reasons behind the low performance of many students of color, English learners, and poor students. Rather than examine school policies and teacher practices, some attribute it to a "culture of poverty" or different community values toward education. The reality is that they struggle not because of their race, language, or poverty. They struggle because we don't offer them sufficient opportunities in the classroom to develop the cognitive skills and habits of mind that would prepare them to take on more advanced academic tasks (Boykin & Noguera, 2011; Jackson, 2011). That's the achievement gap in action. The reasons they are not offered more opportunities for rigor are rooted in the education system's legacy of "separate and unequal" (Kozol, 2006; Oakes, 2005).

School practices that emphasize lecture and rote memorization are part of what Martin Haberman (1991) calls a "pedagogy of poverty" that sets students up to leave high school with outdated skills and shallow knowledge. They are able to regurgitate facts and concepts but have difficulty applying this knowledge in new and practical ways. To be able to direct their own lives and define success for themselves, they must be able to think critically and creatively.

As educators, we have to recognize that we help maintain the achievement gap when we don't teach advanced cognitive skills to students we label as "disadvantaged" because of their language, gender, race, or socioeconomic status. Many children start school with small learning gaps, but as they progress through school, the gap between African American and

Latino and White students grows because we don't teach them how to be independent learners. Based on these labels, we usually do the following (Means & Knapp, 1991):

- Underestimate what disadvantaged students are intellectually capable of doing
- As a result, we postpone more challenging and interesting work until we believe they have mastered "the basics"
- By focusing only on low-level basics, we deprive students of a meaningful or motivating context for learning and practicing higher order thinking processes

Just increasing standards and instructional rigor won't reverse this epidemic. Dependent learners cannot become independent learners by sheer willpower. It is not just a matter of grit or **mindset**. Grit and mindset are necessary but not sufficient by themselves. We have to help dependent students develop new cognitive skills and habits of mind that will actually increase their brainpower. Students with increased brainpower can accelerate their own learning, meaning they know how to learn new content and improve their weak skills on their own.

While the achievement gap has created the epidemic of dependent learners, **culturally responsive teaching** (CRT) is one of our most powerful tools for helping students find their way out of the gap. A systematic approach to culturally responsive teaching is the perfect catalyst to stimulate the brain's neuroplasticity so that it grows new brain cells that help students think in more sophisticated ways.

I define culturally responsive teaching simply as . . .

An educator's ability to recognize students' cultural displays of learning and meaning making and respond positively and constructively with teaching moves that use cultural knowledge as a scaffold to connect what the student knows to new concepts and content in order to promote effective **information processing.** All the while, the educator understands the importance of being in a relationship and having a social-emotional connection to the student in order to create a safe space for learning.

Numerous studies have demonstrated that culturally responsive education can strengthen student connectedness with school and enhance learning (Kalyanpur & Harry, 2012; Tatum, 2009).

There has been a lot written about cultural responsiveness as part of the current reform agenda. As a teacher educator, I see teacher education programs pushing to include cultural responsiveness in their list of competencies for beginning teachers. Many states require teachers to have some type of cross-cultural, language, and academic development (CLAD) certification. Teacher induction programs that support new teachers in their first years in the classroom try to cover the topic in their beginning teacher mentoring programs. Most school districts only offer teachers one-shot professional development "trainings" with little or no continued support. Too often, culturally responsive teaching is promoted as a way to reduce behavior problems or motivate students, while downplaying or ignoring its ability to support rigorous cognitive development.

THE MARRIAGE OF NEUROPLASTICITY AND CULTURALLY RESPONSIVE TEACHING

I can't tell you the number of times someone has asked me for the culturally responsive "cheat sheet" for working with African American, Latino, or even Middle Eastern students. A good number of teachers who have asked me about cultural responsiveness think of it as a "bag of tricks." Far from being a bag of tricks, culturally responsive teaching is a pedagogical approach firmly rooted in learning theory and cognitive science. When used effectively, culturally responsive pedagogy has the ability to help students build **intellective capacity**, also called *fluid intelligence* (Ritchhart, 2002) and *intellective competence* (Gordon, 2001; National Study Group for the Affirmative Development of Academic Ability, 2004). Intellective capacity is the increased power the brain creates to process complex information more effectively. Neuroscience tells us that culture plays a critical role in this process. That's why it is so important for culturally responsive teachers to be well-versed in brain science and cultural understanding.

Beyond knowing the brain science, the biggest challenge I see teachers struggling with is how to operationalize culturally responsive pedagogical principles into culturally responsive teaching practices. It means understanding the basic concepts of culturally responsive pedagogy (Hernandez-Sheets, 2009; Nieto, 2009; Villegas & Lucas, 2002) and then learning the instructional moves associated with them. The Ready for Rigor framework is designed to help teachers do just that with the aid of neuroscience to deepen your understanding (Figure 1.2). This simple framework organizes key areas of teacher capacity building that set the stage for helping students move from being dependent learners to self-directed, independent learners.

Figure 1.2 Ready for Rigor Framework

AWARENESS

- Understand the three levels of culture
- Recognize cultural archetypes of individualism and collectivism
- Understand how the brain learns
- Acknowledge the socio-political context around race and language
- Know and own your cultural lens
- Recognize your brain's triggers around race and culture
- Broaden your interpretation of culturally and linguistically diverse students' learning behaviors

LEARNING PARTNERSHIPS

- Reimagine the student and teacher relationship as a partnership
- Take responsibility to reduce students' social-emotional stress from stereotype threat and microaggressions
- Balance giving students both care and push
- Help students cultivate a positive mindset and sense of self-efficacy
- Support each student to take greater ownership for his learning
  - Give students language to talk about their learning moves

Affirmation · Instructional Conversation · Validation · Wise Feedback

Students are Ready for Rigor and Independent Learning

INFORMATION PROCESSING

- Provide appropriate challenge in order to stimulate brain growth to increase intellective capacity
- Help students process new content using methods from oral traditions
- Connect new content to culturally relevant examples and metaphors from students' community and everyday lives
- Provide students authentic opportunities to process content
- Teach students cognitive routines using the brain's natural learning systems
- Use formative assessments and feedback to increase intellective capacity

COMMUNITY OF LEARNERS AND LEARNING ENVIRONMENT

- Create an environment that is intellectually and socially safe for learning
- Make space for student voice and agency
- Build classroom culture and learning around communal (sociocultural) talk and task structures
- Use classroom rituals and routines to support a culture of learning
- Use principles of restorative justice to manage conflicts and redirect negative behavior

THE FOUR PRACTICE AREAS OF
CULTURALLY RESPONSIVE TEACHING

Learning to put culturally responsive teaching into operation is like learning to rub your head and pat your stomach at the same time. This move feels a bit awkward at first because you have to get your hands to perform two different movements in unison. The trick is to get each movement going independently then synchronizing them into one rhythmic motion. The practices are only effective when done together. In unison they create a synergetic effect. The Ready for Rigor framework lays out four separate practice areas that are interdependent. When the tools and strategies of each area are blended together, they create the social, emotional, and cognitive conditions that allow students to more actively engage and take ownership of their learning process.

The framework is divided into four core areas. The individual components are connected through the principles of brain-based learning:

Practice Area I: Awareness

Successfully teaching students from culturally and linguistically diverse backgrounds—especially students from historically marginalized groups—involves more than just applying specialized teaching techniques. It means placing instruction within the larger sociopolitical context. In this first practice area, we explore the development of our sociopolitical lens. Every culturally responsive teacher develops a sociopolitical consciousness, an understanding that we live in a racialized society that gives unearned privilege to some while others experience unearned disadvantage because of race, gender, class, or language. They are aware of the role that schools play in both perpetuating and challenging those inequities. They are also aware of the impact of their own cultural lens on interpreting and evaluating students' individual or collective behavior that might lead to low expectations or undervaluing the knowledge and skills they bring to school. Mastering this practice area helps teachers

- Locate and acknowledge their own sociopolitical position
- Sharpen and tune their cultural lens
- Learn to manage their own social-emotional response to student diversity

Practice Area II: Learning Partnerships

The second practice area focuses on building trust with students across differences so that the teacher is able to create a social-emotional partnership for deeper learning. Culturally responsive teachers take advantage of the fact that our brains are wired for connection. As they move through the work in this area, teachers build capacity to

- Establish an authentic connection with students that builds mutual trust and respect
- Leverage the trust bond to help students rise to higher expectations
- Give feedback in emotionally intelligent ways so students are able to take it in and act on it
- Hold students to high standards while offering them new intellectual challenges

Practice Area III: Information Processing

The third practice area focuses on knowing how to strengthen and expand students' intellective capacity so that they can engage in deeper, more complex learning. The culturally responsive teacher is the conduit that helps students process what they are learning. They mediate student learning based on what they know about how the brain learns and students' cultural models. This practice area outlines the process, strategies, tactics, and tools for engaging students in high-leverage social and instructional activities that over time build higher order thinking skills. Moving through this area, teachers learn how to

- Understand how culture impacts the brain's information processing
- Orchestrate learning so it builds student's brain power in culturally congruent ways
- Use brain-based information processing strategies common to oral cultures

Practice Area IV: Community Building

In the fourth practice area, we focus on creating an environment that feels socially and intellectually safe for dependent learners to stretch themselves and take risks. Too often, we think of the physical setup of our classroom as being culturally "neutral" when in reality it is often an extension of the teacher's worldview or the dominant culture. The culturally responsive teacher tries to create an environment that communicates care, support, and belonging in ways that students recognize. As they move through this practice area, teachers understand how to

- Integrate universal cultural elements and themes into the classroom
- Use cultural practices and orientations to create a socially and intellectually safe space
- Set up rituals and routines that reinforce self-directed learning and academic identity

CHAPTER SUMMARY

- The achievement gap has denied underserved students of color and English learners opportunities to develop the cognitive skills and processes that help them become independent learners.
- Culturally responsive teaching is a powerful tool to help dependent learners develop the cognitive skills for higher order thinking.
- Culturally responsive teaching uses the brain principles from neuroscience to mediate learning effectively.
- The Ready for Rigor framework helps us operationalize culturally responsive teaching.

INVITATION TO INQUIRY

- How is your school addressing the needs of low-performing students of color?
- How do you support struggling students to become independent learners?
- How have you and your colleagues operationalized the principles of culturally responsive teaching?

GOING DEEPER

To deepen your knowledge, here are some books, reports, and articles I would recommend:

- *All Students Reaching the Top: Strategies for Closing Academic Achievement Gaps* by the National Study Group for the Affirmative Development of Academic Ability.
- *The Flat World and Education: How America's Commitment to Equity Will Determine Our Future* by Linda Darling-Hammond.

What's Culture   **2**
Got to Do with It?

Understanding the
Deep Roots of Culture

Preservation of one's own culture does not require contempt or disrespect for other cultures.

—Cesar Chavez, Mexican American Activist

We often talk about the problem of the achievement gap in terms of race—racial relations, issues of oppression and equity—while ironically the solutions for closing students' learning gaps in the classroom lie in tapping into their culture. But just why and how we use culture to close learning gaps remains vague for many teachers and seems counterintuitive for others who may have been taught not to focus on differences and, instead, be "color-blind." The question—what's culture got to do with it?—is an important one culturally responsive teachers need to be able to answer. In this chapter, we highlight the first practice area of the Ready for Rigor framework: *Awareness.* Just as students need to have rich background for comprehension and problem solving, teachers need adequate background knowledge and usable information in order to know how to apply culturally responsive tools and strategies. Building background knowledge begins with becoming knowledgeable about the dimensions of culture as well as knowledgeable about the larger social, political, and economic conditions that create inequitable education outcomes. In addition to awareness of how culture is constructed or the impact of larger social and political forces on learning, teachers also have to be aware of their beliefs regarding equity and culture. Building background knowledge and awareness is one of the critical objectives of the first practice area of the framework.

UNDERSTANDING CULTURE

Culture, it turns out, is the way that every brain makes sense of the world. That is why everyone, regardless of race or ethnicity, has a culture. Think of culture as software for the brain's hardware. The brain uses cultural information to turn everyday happenings into meaningful events. If we want to help dependent learners do more higher order thinking and problem solving, then we have to access their brain's cognitive structures to deliver culturally responsive instruction.

So, in this chapter, we start with building our awareness of the three levels of culture.

Levels of Culture

Culture operates on a surface level, an intermediate or shallow level, and a deep level.

Surface culture

This level is made up of observable and concrete elements of culture such as food, dress, music, and holidays. This level of culture has a low emotional charge so that changes don't create great anxiety in a person or group.

Shallow culture

This level is made up of the unspoken rules around everyday social interactions and norms, such as courtesy, attitudes toward elders, nature of friendship, concepts of time, personal space between people, nonverbal communication, rules about eye contact, or appropriate touching. It's at this level of culture that we put into action our deep cultural values. Nonverbal communication that builds **rapport** and trust between people comes out of shallow culture. This level has a strong emotional charge. At the same time, at this level we interpret certain behaviors as disrespectful, offensive, or hostile. Social violation of norms at this level can cause mistrust, distress, or social friction.

Deep culture

This level is made up of tacit knowledge and unconscious assumptions that govern our worldview. It also contains the cosmology (view of good or bad) that guides ethics, spirituality, health, and theories of group harmony (i.e., competition or cooperation). Deep culture also governs how we learn new information. Elements at this level have an intense emotional charge. **Mental models** at this level help the brain interpret threats or rewards in the environment. Challenges to cultural values at this level produce culture shock or trigger the brain's fight or flight response.

At the deep cultural level, our brain is encoding itself with the particular worldview we will carry into our formative years. Two people from different cultures can look at the same event and have very different reactions to it because of the meaning they attach to the event based on their deep culture. For example, in Eastern culture, the color red means good luck while in most Western cultures red means danger. While every person's individual culture evolves as we grow up and experience the world, our core mental models stay with us. My grandmother had a saying, "you can take the boy out of the country but you can't take the country out of the boy." The point is that one's culture, especially one's deep cultural roots, is part of how the brain makes sense of the world and helps us function in our environment. This worldview continues to guide our behaviors even when we change our geography. We call these mental models **schema**.

Think of mental models as parts of an elaborate "tree of knowledge" inside our brains. Schema represent the pieces of inert information we've taken in, interpreted, and categorized, based on our deep cultural norms, beliefs, and ways of being. Schema help us create background knowledge or what researcher Luis Moll and his colleagues (2005) call *funds of knowledge*, the "historically accumulated and culturally developed bodies of knowledge and skills essential for household or individual functioning and well-being" (p. 133). Another way of understanding schema is to think of it as a set of conceptual scripts that guide our comprehension of the world. For example, think about going to a restaurant. By just thinking about it, you activated your schema for restaurants. Images, smells, tastes, experiences involving food, how to order, and how to behave in that environment come immediately to mind without any effort. We make sense of the world around us by creating these schema scripts based on our deep culture. They are the brain's software that directs its hardware.

When talking about culture, people often represent the three levels of culture as an iceberg, with surface culture as the tip of the iceberg, shallow culture located just below the water line, and deep culture the largest

Figure 2.1 Culture Tree

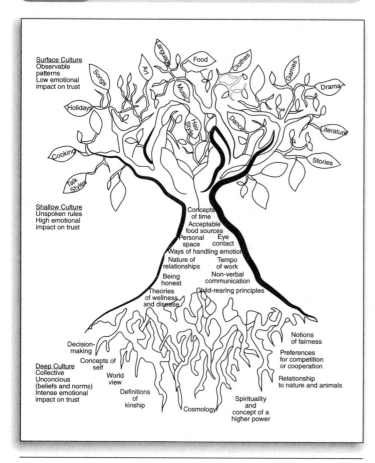

Source: Illustration by Aliza Maynard.

part hidden deep in the water. Rather than use the metaphor of an iceberg, I like to compare culture to a tree. A tree is part of a bigger ecosystem that shapes and impacts its growth and development. Shallow culture is represented in the trunk and branches of the tree while we can think of surface culture as the observable fruit that the tree bears. Surface and shallow culture are not static; they change and shift over time as social groups move around and ethnic groups intermarry, resulting in a cultural mosaic just as branches and fruit on a tree change in response to the seasons and its environment. Deep culture is like the root system of a tree. It is what grounds the individual and nourishes his mental health. It is the bedrock of self-concept, group identity, approaches to problem solving, and decision making.

BUT I HAVE 19 DIFFERENT CULTURES IN MY CLASSROOM!

"I have 19 different cultures represented in my classroom. Do I have to learn about the customs, foods, and beliefs of 19 different cultures?" This is the question I always get from teachers new to culturally responsive teaching. The key to understanding how culture guides the brain during culturally responsive teaching lies in focusing on deep culture. Rather than focus on the visible "fruits" of culture—dress, food, holidays, and heroes—we have to focus on the roots of culture: worldview, core beliefs, and group values. The answer to this question comes from understanding universal patterns across cultures. I call these similarities **cultural archetypes**. While cultures might be different at the surface and shallow levels, at the root of different cultures there are common values, world-views, and practices that form these archetypes. The term *archetype* has its origins in ancient Greek. It comes from the root word *archein*, which means "original or old" and the word *typos*, which means "pattern, model, or type." While there might be a number of different cultures represented in one's classroom, when we look closer, we see patterns that unite some cultures. Understanding these cultural archetypes can make culturally responsive teaching more manageable in a diverse classroom. Cultural archetypes give us a starting point.

Cultural Archetypes

There are two cultural archetypes that I think are important for the culturally responsive teacher to know.

Collectivism and Individualism

A common cultural archetype connected with deep culture is a group's orientation toward either collectivism or individualism (Figure 2.2). Collectivism and individualism reflect fundamentally different ways the brain organizes itself. Turns out our brains are wired to favor a communal view of the world. Humans have always sought to be in community with each other because it enhanced our chances of survival. We shared workloads and resources. Over time, our brains became hardwired toward working and living cooperatively. As people moved from rural communities to urban communities, they became less communal and more individualistic. Dutch sociologist, Geert Hofstede found that approximately 20% of the world has an individualistic culture, while the other 80% practice a collectivist culture (Hofstede, Hofstede, & Minkov, 2010). Most European cultures were rooted in an individualistic mindset, while the collectivist worldview is common among Latin American, Asian, African, Middle Eastern, and many Slavic cultures (Figure 2.3). Collectivistic societies emphasize relationships, interdependence within a community, and cooperative learning. Individualistic societies emphasize individual achievement and independence.

In America, the dominant culture is individualistic, while the cultures of many African American, Latino, Pacific Islander, and Native American communities lean more toward collectivism. Across these communities, how collectivism is expressed varies. What might be acceptable in one

Figure 2.2 Features of Individualist and Collectivist Cultures

Individualism	Collectivism
Focused on independence and individual achievement	Focused on interdependence and group success
Emphasizes self-reliance and the belief that one is supposed to take care of himself to get ahead	Emphasizes reliance on the collective wisdom or resources of the group and the belief that group members take care of each other to get ahead
Learning happens through individual study and reading	Learning happens through group interaction and dialogue
Individual contributions and status are important	Group dynamics and harmony are important
Competitive	Collaborative
Technical/Analytical	Relational

collectivist-oriented community might not be acceptable in another. What does stay the same is the focus on relationships and cooperative learning.

I don't want to stereotype cultures into an oversimplified frame but to simply offer the archetypes of collectivism and individualism as a way of understanding the general cultural orientation among diverse students in the classroom. We recognize that individualism and collectivism exist on a continuum. Some cultures are individualistic with little or no collectivistic elements, while others might be primarily collectivistic with strong elements of individualism. It is simply a starting point for building on the shared culture of your students.

Review Hofstede's list in Figure 2.3 and notice the difference between the United States' highly individualistic dominant culture and the highly collectivist cultures of many Latin and African countries, where our students have their roots. For example, the United States has an individualism index of 91 out of 100, meaning our dominant cultural messages and norms revolve around a self-reliance "pull yourself up by your bootstraps" mindset, with a strong focus on competition and self-promotion. On the other hand, a country such as Guatemala with an individualism index of 6 leans more toward a communal culture that downplays self-promotion in favor of promoting harmony and interdependence in the family or workplace above all else. One can see there is a cultural mismatch between the typical American culture that's focused on individual personal achievement and recognition and the typical Guatemalan culture that puts a premium on being in a positive relationship with others as a foundation for business, learning, and social interaction.

Figure 2.3 The Individualism-Collectivism Continuum

The Cultural Dimensions Index was created by cultural psychologist, Geert Hofstede. Countries are evaluated on a 100-point scale in seven dimensions. One dimension is the level of individualism within a society. At the high end of the scale are extremely individualist cultures (self-oriented, individual effort favored in business and learning, competition over cooperation) while a lower number signals a more collectivist culture (group orientation, relationships essential to business and learning, and cooperation over competition).

Country	Score	Country	Score
United States	91	United Arab Emirates	38
Australia	90	Turkey	37
United Kingdom	89	Uruguay	36
Netherlands	80	Greece	35
New Zealand	79	Philippines	32
Italy	76	Mexico	30
Belgium	75	Tanzania	27
Denmark	74	Ethiopia	27
France	71	Kenya	27
Sweden	71	Portugal	27
Ireland	70	Zambia	27
Norway	69	Malaysia	26
Switzerland	68	Hong Kong	25
Germany	67	Chile	23
South Africa	65	China	20
Finland	63	Ghana	20
Poland	60	Nigeria	20
Czech Republic	58	Sierra Leone	20
Austria	55	Singapore	20
Hungary	55	Thailand	20
Israel	54	El Salvador	19
Spain	51	South Korea	18
India	48	Taiwan	17
Argentina	41	Peru	16
Japan	41	Costa Rica	15
Iran	41	Indonesia	14
Jamaica	39	Pakistan	14
Brazil	38	Colombia	13
Egypt	38	Venezuela	12
Iraq	38	Panama	11
Kuwait	38	Ecuador	8
Lebanon	38	Guatemala	6
Saudi Arabia	38		

Source: Hofstede, G., Hofstede, G. J., & Minkov, M. (2010). *Cultures and organizations: Software of the mind.* New York: McGraw-Hill.

Oral and Written Traditions

Two other important cultural archetypes to keep in mind are written and oral traditions. Some cultures have relied on the spoken word rather than the written word to convey, preserve, and reproduce knowledge from generation to generation. By telling stories and coding knowledge into songs, chants, proverbs, and poetry, groups with a strong oral tradition record and sustain their cultures and cultural identities by word of mouth. The oral tradition places a heavy emphasis on relationships because the process connects the speaker and listener in a communal experience. In contrast, a written tradition does not require much person-to-person interaction or dialogue because thoughts are committed to print.

In addition, an oral tradition makes the most of the brain's memory systems by using alliteration, movement, and emotion as strong cognitive anchors. Performance-based practices such as dancing and drumming are also used to encode knowledge.

Although most oral cultures now use reading and writing as tools for documentation and communication in formal settings, many still rely on their oral traditions at home and in their immediate communities. This situation reinforces the brain's preference for processing information through traditional oral methods.

NAMING THE SOCIOPOLITICAL CONTEXT

In addition to recognizing the cultural archetypes operating among culturally and linguistically diverse students, the culturally responsive teacher also has to be able to name and acknowledge the larger sociopolitical context schools operate within. Teacher educators, Villegas and Lucas (2002) identified six characteristics of culturally responsive educators and put understanding the sociopolitical context as one of the most important. The **sociopolitical context** is a term used to describe the series of mutually reinforcing policies and practices across social, economic, and political domains that contribute to disparities and unequal opportunities for people of color in housing, transportation, education, and health care, to name a few. These unequal opportunities result in unequal outcomes along racial and class lines.

For example, we see redlining by banks that make it nearly impossible for people living in predominately Black communities to get a mortgage because of income, or gerrymandering of political districts to reduce the political influence of communities of color, or the dumping of toxic wastes in low-income communities that contribute to high cancer mortality rates because there is no access to quality health care. According to Kirwan Institute for the Study of Race and Ethnicity (2013), there are two key components of the sociopolitical context: *implicit racial bias* and *structural racialization.* Together they reinforce each other like bookends and hold a system of inequality in place that doesn't require overt racism or any racist actors at all to maintain it. As a result, inequality doesn't look like the Jim Crow laws of the pre–Civil Rights era. Instead, it takes the form of seemingly benign institutional practices or structures that reduce and limit opportunities for people of color, poor people, and immigrants.

Implicit bias refers to the unconscious attitudes and stereotypes that shape our responses to certain groups. Implicit bias operates involuntarily, often without one's awareness or intentional control, which is different from explicit racism. It is important to understand that implicit bias is not just overt racism that's hidden on purpose. Implicit bias is not implicit racism. Why we engage in implicit bias is rooted in neuroscience and related to our brain's efforts to process large amounts of incoming data by using its shortcut we know as stereotyping. Even educators who have taken an explicit social justice or progressive stance have implicit bias based on their exposure to the dominant culture's messages and memes over a lifetime. In the next chapter, we will learn more about how the brain does this, but what's important here to recognize is that implicit bias is directly related to how our brains are wired and seems so "normal" that these bias messages often go unchecked within the larger society (Kirwan Institute, 2013).

The other bookend holding the sociopolitical context in place is **structural racialization**. If we look at our society as a complex system of organizations, institutions, individuals, processes, and policies, we can see how many factors interact to create and perpetuate social, economic, and political structures that are harmful to people of color and to our society as a whole. Housing, education, and health are just a few areas where distribution of material resources, quality of service, and access still result in opportunity being distributed along racial lines. Understanding structural racialization goes beyond finding intent—proof of racism—within our social, economic, political, and medical institutions. Structural racialization is deeply connected to the relationship between where one lives and how location and geography affect one's access to education and job opportunities, as well as other quality-of-life factors.

To understand structural racialization, we have to move beyond one-dimensional, linear explanations of inequity in society and education.

We have to entertain the idea that a series of seemingly benign or supposedly well-intended policies actually create a negative cumulative and reinforcing effect that supports, rather than dismantles, the status quo within institutions. The impact of structural racialization across institutions over time creates a domino effect that leads to unearned disadvantages that obscure the real source of the inequity. For example, prior to No Child Left Behind, school districts across the country were concerned with the fact that, in the United States, African American students were not performing as well as White students on standardized tests. The statement was factually correct. So we designed No Child Left Behind to focus on closing the gap in test scores between Black and White students because we believed we needed to help children of color and English learners better prepare for the test. So "teaching to the test" to cover subject matter content better became the primary focus in many classrooms.

Still more than a decade later the achievement gap persists, especially with regard to students' ability to do higher order analytical work. Our focus was on helping students become better test takers rather than on looking at the interplay of social and institutional practices that negatively impact African American children so that they didn't develop the skills to do independent learning or higher order thinking, both of which are needed to excel on standardized tests.

Policy makers were not willing to look beyond that overly simplistic symptom of the achievement gap, test scores. Research findings pointed to the domino effect resulting from the lack of federally funded quality childcare and preschool for children of color, 0–5 years old living in urban and rural communities. We know quality daycare and preschool experiences contribute to optimum brain growth and rich vocabulary development. Access to quality daycare, child and maternal health services, and jobs that paid a living wage all contribute to children starting school academically and socially ready. The Harlem Children's Zone, with its comprehensive approach to health, education, and job development, was actually set up as a direct response to the structural racialization that negatively impacted children in that community long before they went to school.

Structural racialization doesn't happen just outside of school. The school-to-prison pipeline is actually a manifestation of structural racialization. We see it in the way we make staffing decisions in education. Often, underresourced urban schools are staffed by new teachers or teachers deemed "less effective" (Education Trust, 2006). Highly effective teachers are "rewarded" with teaching assignments to high performing schools or gifted and talented classes. We routinely put the less experienced teachers with the neediest students. No other profession does this. A challenging medical case gets the attention of top specialists and skilled surgeons. It would be considered malpractice to put someone unskilled or new to the profession on a complicated medical case. Yet, in education, we subject our neediest dependent learners to inadequate instruction given their needs, or we allow them to lose valuable instructional time because of questionable discipline practices. As a result, culturally and linguistically diverse students don't develop the skills, vocabulary, or background knowledge necessary to be ready for rigor.

We see this acutely in the area of reading. By third grade, many culturally and linguistically diverse students are one or more years behind in reading. We know that each year they will fall further behind in both advanced reading skills and content knowledge because of the system's failure to prevent or close small learning gaps in earlier grades. By middle school, most schools don't know how to address struggling seventh and eighth graders with basic decoding and low fluency problems in reading.

Over time, because of structural racialization in education, we have seen a new type of intellectual apartheid happening in schools, creating dependent learners who cannot access the curriculum and independent learners who have had the opportunity to build the cognitive skills to do deep learning on their own. Rather than stepping back, looking at the ways we structure inequity in education, and interrupting these practices, we simply focus on creating short-term solutions to get dependent students of color to score high on each year's standardized tests. We don't focus on building their intellective capacity so that they can begin to fill their own learning gaps with proper scaffolding.

SOCIOPOLITICAL CONTEXT VERSUS THE CULTURE OF POVERTY

Some educators confuse the concept of the sociopolitical context with the popular notion of a culture of poverty. As a part of being aware as a culturally responsive teacher it is critical to understand the difference. I bumped up against this confusion during a monthly seminar my colleague and I were leading for a group of 60 BTSA (Beginning Teacher Support Assessment) support providers at the Santa Clara Office of Education in California. That month's seminar focused on how to coach beginning teachers to be culturally responsive. I was explaining how signs of affirmation can show up even in kindergarten classrooms by making sure that there are simple things on hand such as multicultural crayons and construction paper. A hand quickly shot up. A veteran teacher and long time BTSA support provider said that she thought a better strategy would be to teach "these low-income kids" to mix the crayons instead because they won't have these special multicultural crayons at home because their parents don't invest in educational supplies. I was a bit stunned by her comment. After I took a few deep breaths to calm myself, I asked her what she based her suggestion on. She told me she'd learned this from Ruby Payne's framework for teaching children in poverty. Poor people, she'd learned, are really resourceful because that's part of their culture of poverty. Several others in the room nodded.

As a learning community, we took some time to unpack the difference between the culture of poverty and the sociopolitical context. Paul Gorski of EdChange (2008) offers an insightful commentary on the myth of the culture of poverty. He suggests that the idea of a culture of poverty reinforces stereotypes of poor families, a disproportionate number who are families of color, as unmotivated, not caring about education, or involved in illegal activities as a lifestyle choice. There's considerable research that clearly states that people in poverty are not, in fact, lazier, less likely to value education, or more likely to be substance abusers than their wealthier counterparts. Yet, implicit racial bias reinforces the notion of people of color willingly living in poverty or unmotivated to change their circumstances. This view ignores the contributing factors of structural racialization in society that limit a family's economic and educational opportunities. Culturally responsive teachers acknowledge the impact of the sociopolitical context on children of color and their families.

Here are three key points we need to keep in mind regarding this so-called culture of poverty:

Poverty is not a culture. Most families are trapped in poverty and do not willingly embrace it as a way of life. Most poor families experience generational poverty because of the lack of opportunities for moving out of poverty. Most poor families hold down at least one full-time job. We call these families the working poor. In economics, they refer to it as the *cycle of poverty*—a set of factors or events by which poverty, once started, is likely to continue unless there is strong outside intervention. The cycle of poverty has been defined as a phenomenon where poor families become trapped in poverty for at least three generations (i.e., for enough time that the family includes no surviving ancestors who possess and can transmit the intellectual, social, and cultural capital necessary to stay out of or escape poverty).

It is a condition or symptom of the structural inequities built into our social and economic systems. Poverty for most families is not a lifestyle choice. Poverty doesn't fit the definition of culture in that it doesn't have deep cultural roots governed by a cosmology or worldview.

Coping skills are mistaken for norms and beliefs. What appears to be a "culture"—norms, beliefs, and behaviors that are transmitted from one generation to another—are more accurately coping and survival mechanisms that help marginalized communities navigate what Alexander in *The New Jim Crow* calls racial and economic caste systems. The experience of African Americans and Latinos living in poverty is no different than the experience of those living through the Great Depression or major military conflicts. The only difference is those experiences were temporary, so the coping mechanisms did not become codified.

Poor people do not normalize or glorify negative aspects of living in poverty. Despite images we commonly see in the popular media, behaviors such as drug use, violence, or out of wedlock births are not normalized and embraced as lifestyle choices by poor people. Often these behaviors are an outgrowth of post-traumatic stress disorder (PTSD). Dr. Victor Carrion and his colleagues (2007) of Stanford's Early Life Stress Research Program point out that as many as one-third of children living in our country's urban neighborhoods have PTSD—nearly twice the rate reported for troops returning from war zones in Iraq.

The primary reason I think the idea of a culture of poverty is incompatible with culturally responsive teaching is because it promotes deficit thinking. Deficit thinking defines students and their families by their weaknesses rather than their strengths, suggesting that these weaknesses stem from low intelligence, poor moral character, or inadequate social skills. At its core, the culture of poverty theory says that poor people are responsible for their lot in life because of their individual and collective deficiencies (Collins, 1988). It does not acknowledge the impact of institutionalized racism, structural racialization, skin color privilege, or language discrimination.

IMPLICATIONS FOR MOVING DEPENDENT LEARNERS AND BUILDING INTELLECTIVE CAPACITY

Understanding culture, recognizing cultural archetypes, and recognizing the sociopolitical context are about laying the foundation for being a culturally responsive teacher. Recognizing how we have created intellectual apartheid in schools is the first step in knowing how to build intellective capacity. Getting dependent students of color ready for rigor begins with our awareness of current reality and acknowledgment of our past racial history. This understanding will give us a better context for supporting the social-emotional needs of dependent learners.

CHAPTER SUMMARY

- Deep culture, not the heroes and holidays of surface culture is at the core of culturally responsive teaching. Culture acts as our brain's software.
- One of the key ways to reduce confusion about how to attend to all the different cultures represented in my classroom is to first identify which cultural archetype dominates—individualism or collectivism.
- The themes of relationships and group interdependence are central to collectivist culture. Collectivist values and practices are expressed differently within different collectivist cultures.
- Culture isn't the only thing that needs to be considered when planning for culturally responsive teaching. The sociopolitical context also shapes the needs of culturally and linguistically diverse students.
- Implicit bias and structural racialization are current realities that undergird life opportunities for families of color. Structural racialization doesn't require racist actors to be true.
- There are several urban myths about the culture of poverty that have become memes in education.

INVITATION TO INQUIRY

- What would you say are the cultural archetypes operating among your students? What cultural practices do you see enacted?
- Become observant about how individualism and collectivism are operating in your classroom or school community.
- How do you experience structural racialization? How do you believe your students experience it? What differences do you notice?

GOING DEEPER

- *Bridging Cultures Between Home and School: A Guide for Teachers* (2001) by Elise Trumbull, Carrie Rothstein-Fisch, Patricia M. Greenfield, and Blanca Quiroz

- *The Light in Their Eyes: Creating Multicultural Learning Communities,* 10th Anniversary Edition (2009) by Sonia Nieto
- *Con Respeto: Bridging the Distances Between Culturally Diverse Families and Schools* (1996) by Guadelupe Valdes
- Kirwan Institute for the Study of Race and Ethnicity. *State of the Science: Review of Implicit Bias Research Findings.* Retrieved from: http://kirwaninstitute.osu.edu/wp-content/uploads/2014/03/2014-implicit-bias.pdf
- Harlem Children's Zone. CBS *60 Minutes* (2009). Retrieved from: https://www.youtube.com/watch?v=Di0-xN6xc_w

3 This Is Your Brain on Culture

Understanding How Culture Programs The Brain

> *Culture is the widening of the mind and of the spirit.*
>
> —Jawaharlal Nehru, first Prime Minister of India

In the last chapter, I introduced you to the three levels of culture with a focus on the deepest level of values, norms, and beliefs rather than the surface elements, such as food, dress, music, and holidays. We looked at two important *cultural archetypes*—individualism and collectivism—as a way to organize culture in our minds at a macro level. And last, I talked about how implicit bias influences structural racialization and the larger sociopolitical context. In this chapter, we continue to explore the Practice Area of Awareness in the Ready for Rigor framework as we build important background knowledge about how the brain uses culture at all three levels to make sense of the world. We will also look at how our cultural programming contributes to implicit bias.

If we want to use culturally responsive teaching to support the cognitive development of dependent learners, we have to know how the brain uses culture to make sense of the world. When we know this, we can easily piggyback on the brain's natural systems to activate its unique ability to grow itself.

I want to give you a heads up about this chapter. We are going to take a quick, deep dive into the brain's physical structures. It can feel a bit technical, but it's necessary in order to establish a foundation for culturally responsive teaching. Here's an image to hold on to that might help. Think of the physical structures we are about to examine as the brain's hardware and culture as the software that programs it. Just like our computers, all brains come with a default setting that acts as its prime directive regardless of race, class, language, or culture: *Avoid threats to safety at all costs and seek well-being at every opportunity.* Neuroscientists have long known that our brains are wired to keep us alive at all costs. Our deep cultural values program our brain on how to interpret the world around us—what a real threat looks like and what will bring a sense of security.

THE PHYSICAL STRUCTURES OF THE BRAIN

Let's begin with an overview of the brain's "hardware," namely its physical structures. These basic structures are important to understand before we look at culture and the brain. From the time our human ancestor was trying to avoid lions on the savanna and foraging for edible plants, the brain continued to evolve into a complex learning machine, recording and cataloguing information through experience and then changing itself so that it knew which situations to avoid and which ones to seek out quickly.

The complex architecture of our brains developed in three layers, from the bottom up, like the floors of a house. Each one is layered on top of the other, with the first layer being the oldest. Each is powerful in its own unique way. Keep in mind that these three parts of the brain do not operate independently of one another. Instead, they do a synchronized dance. They communicate by sending electromagnetic and chemical messages back and forth. In addition to their own dance, they work in unison with the body's nervous system.

The Reptilian Region

The first brain layer is the reptilian region. It is 500 million years old. It's nicknamed the "lizard brain" because it's made up of the same two structures found in the entire reptilian brain: the brainstem and the cerebellum. It doesn't think. It only reacts. It is always on, even when we are sleeping. The lizard brain allows you to smell smoke or hear a loud suspicious noise when you are asleep. It is what wakes you up. The brain stem is the structure that connects the brain to the spinal cord. Its

Figure 3.1 Cross Section of Brain with Labels

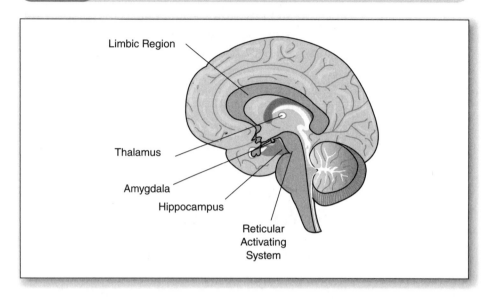

primary function is to keep our body alive. It controls automatic functions, such as breathing, heartbeat, body temperature, digestion, blood pressure, and balance. It is able to increase heartbeat, blood flow, and other automatic body functions if it gets signals that danger is near, or it can slow down responses if we are just chilling out with friends. It also houses the **reticular activating system** (RAS), a critical brain feature that's responsible for alertness and attention. Using the RAS, the brain scans our surroundings 24/7 for any *novelty* that signals important changes in the environment, any *relevant* event or information connected to one's social status, physical survival, or strong *emotions* that might signal a potential threat or reward. Getting the RAS to pay attention is critical in culturally responsive teaching. It directs the learner's attention at the beginning of a task.

The Limbic Region

Stacked right on top of the reptilian region is the limbic layer. This layer is only present in mammals. It is also called the emotional brain. This region links emotions, behavior, and cognition together (Zull, 2002). Its primary roles are to help us learn from experience, manage our emotions, and remember. The limbic brain records memories of experiences and behaviors that produced positive and negative results in the past, so a person knows what threats to avoid or what rewards to pursue. It creates our internal schema that acts as our background knowledge.

Figure 3.2 Three Critical Limbic Brain Functions

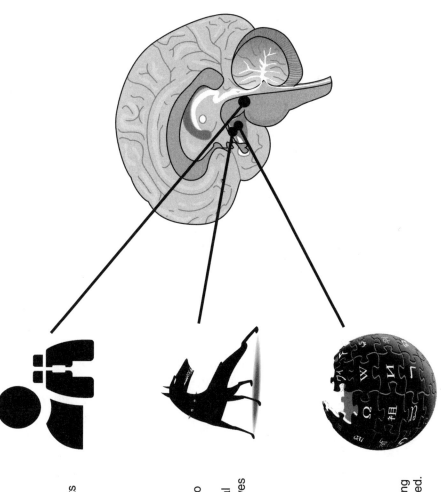

The Watcher
(Reticular Activating System)

The RAS scans our environment 24/7 for possible threats (bodily harm or humiliation) or rewards (food or friendship). It sends reports over to the amygdala.

The Guard Dog
(Amygdala)

The amygdala acts as our guard dog trained to prepare the body for fight, flight, freeze, or appease when anything threatens our physical or social safety. It can act on its own if it believes we are in imminent danger.

The Wikipedia Pages
(Hippocampus)

The hippocampus is our personal Wikipedia. Here is where our background knowledge is stored. It is also the site of working memory, where information processing happens. Working memory shrinks when the amygdala is triggered.

There are three specific structures of the limbic brain that help it manage memories and emotions. Each is a key player in effective learning:

- *Thalamus.* It acts as the brain's communication dispatch hub. All incoming sensory information that the RAS lets in passes through the thalamus (except smell) and then is directed to other parts of the brain for additional processing.
- *Hippocampus.* It acts as the brain's background knowledge data bank. It houses the memory system—**short-term memory**, which holds information for as little as 5–20 seconds and the **working memory** that holds information for up to 20 minutes. Working memory is where the brain "works" to connect new information to old knowledge in order to turn facts, figures, dates, concepts, or skills into something that has meaning and relevance to the learner (Bransford, Brown, & Cocking, 2000; Sousa, 2001). This is where active learning takes place. **Long-term memory** is where our background knowledge is stored. Think of long-term memory as our own personal Wikipedia pages, always open for reference in order to help us make sense of what's going on around us.
- *Amygdala.* It acts as the brain's guard dog. The amygdala is an almond-shaped structure deep inside the limbic layer of the brain. It is the seat of our fear system that is involved in emotional processing. It is designed to react in less than a second at the very hint of a social or physical threat. It has the "authority" to bypass the brain's communication dispatch hub in the thalamus and send distress signals directly to the lizard brain in the form of the stress hormone **cortisol**. We call this bypass an **amygdala hijack**. When the amygdala sounds its alarm with cortisol, all other cognitive functions such as learning, problem solving, or creative thinking stop. An amygdala hijack leads to our natural "fight, flight, freeze, or appease" responses.

The Neocortex Region

The newest brain layer of the brain is only 3–4 million years old. Compared to the reptilian region, it is slow in processing information but really, really smart. It is home to our *executive function.* Executive function is the command center of the brain. It oversees our thinking and manages our working memory. It controls planning, abstract thinking, organization, and self-regulation. It also houses our imagination.

In addition to executive function, the neocortex has an almost endless capacity to learn and rewire itself. For example, an infant's brain is born capable of speaking over 3,000 human languages, but it is not born proficient in any of them. When the baby begins to hear his new home language, his brain begins to catalogue the sounds of that particular language. Over a short period of time, the baby's brain begins to hardwire itself so that it selectively strengthens the language networks that reproduce the specific sounds and grammatical patterns he hears his parents using. At the same time, his brain begins to prune the nerve connections for sounds and grammatical patterns that aren't used in his home language (Sylwester, 1995).

It is here in the neocortex that we have the chance to build our brain power, also called our intellective capacity. The challenge is getting past the lower brain's two emotional gatekeepers: the reticular activating system (RAS) and the amygdala.

PAUSE TO PROCESS

Let's pause here for a minute to process what we learned about the brain's physical structures so far.

First, consider these questions:

- What did you read that squared with your understanding?
- What questions are going around in your head about how the brain structures interact?
- What three points stood out for you? Why?

Next, for a little practice, try describing in your own words how the three parts of the limbic brain interact or try explaining the relationship of the amygdala to the RAS. Imagine you have to explain these processes to a fifth grader. How would you describe them?

Cellular Structures

The next brain structures that are important for us to know are too small to see with the naked eye but are critical to building intellective capacity. The cellular structures are made up of special nerves called **neurons** that are the brain's building blocks. Neurons are so small that 30,000 neurons can fit on a pinhead. Neurons are the messengers that carry information back and forth across each region of the brain. The brain contains tens of billions of neurons. They are that stuff we call **gray matter** in the brain. Here's a fun fact. There is not a fixed amount of gray matter in the brain like the 1.5 gallons of blood we have running through our bodies. Because of **neuroplasticity**, the brain is able to grow an unlimited amount of gray matter in response to our continuous learning. That's why the brain appears all wrinkled and folded into itself. Those folds and wrinkles represent a person's capacity to do complex thinking and problem solving. It's the only place on the body where wrinkles are a good thing.

Learning happens as the neurons communicate with each other much like runners in a relay race. Think of the information being learned as the baton that the relay runners pass along to each other. Within the neuron, the baton takes the form of electrical impulses and chemical interactions. We call this process "firing." These impulses travel along the long *axon*, which is an extension of the neuron until it connects with another neuron. They exchange information through the short, fingerlike extensions called **dendrites**. The dendrites contain receptors that extend out beyond the body of the neuron to pick up messages from other neurons. The more dendrites we have, the more information that the neurons can pick up and

Figure 3.3 Picture of Neuron with Axon and Dendrites

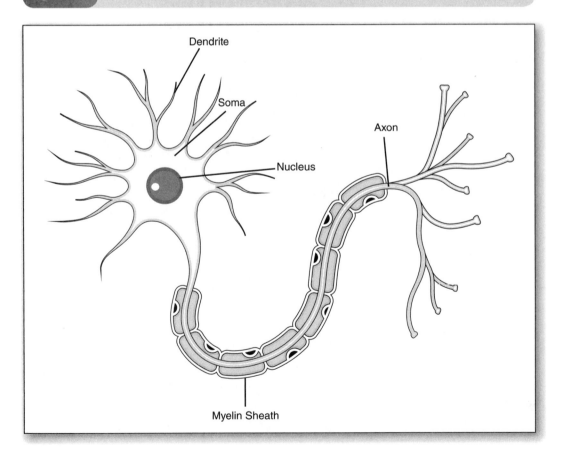

pass along. The brain signals the neurons to grow more dendrites in response to new cognitive challenges, novel problem solving, and increased physical activity so it can do more complex information processing.

When the brain is learning something new it clusters neurons together to create a *neural pathway,* similar to a footpath through a forest. Neural pathways are important because when we go back and forth along this pathway when thinking or problem solving, it helps drive new learning deeper into long-term memory until it becomes automatic or deeply understood. When neurons in different regions of the brain "fire" together during a learning task, the pathways are linked and strengthened, leading to stronger and deeper learning. The saying among neuroscientists is that "neurons that fire together, wire together." This is an important point we will come back to again in Chapter 8 when we look at information processing.

The brain helps neurons talk to each other faster along these neural pathways through the process of **myelination**, where it wraps the body of the neuron with layers of a fatty substance called **myelin**. Myelination makes it easier for the brain to do more complex work because the fat allows the chemical and electrical impulses to travel across the neuron faster. Repetition or deliberate practice of a specific move, such as practicing free throws from the three-point line, perfecting a challenging finger position on the violin, memorizing important content, doing a complex puzzle, or reciting a poem over and over to commit it to memory, triggers the release of myelin, and initiates the wrapping process. Think of myelination as the difference between having a high speed broadband wireless internet connection and a slow dial-up connection (Coyle, 2009). We all know what that's like.

Conversely, when we don't practice or use new dendrites shortly after a learning episode, our brain prunes them by starving them and then reabsorbing them. It assumes that if you didn't revisit the activity that grew the dendrites that information wasn't important to keep. The footpath gets overgrown and disappears, making it hard to find your way back to stored knowledge and skills.

PAUSE TO PROCESS

When we talk about neuroplasticity that grows a student's intellective capacity, we are talking about this process of growing dendrites, creating neural pathways, and initiating myelination.

What analogies or metaphors might you use to describe the process of growing neurons and dendrites?

The Nervous System

The last brain structure to understand is the nervous system. Most of us have this image of the brain as a superprocessing machine. We are always impressed with its computerlike functions when we talk about how fast it can multitask—pumping blood, checking blood pressure, digesting food, all the while walking, noticing the beautiful sunset, and keeping an eye on the dog we just let off the leash.

Despite its impressive technical capabilities, the brain is a social organ, meaning it works best when it has the opportunity to connect and interact with others (Hanson, 2013; Zull, 2002). That is where the body's nervous system comes in. The nervous system is just an extension of the other brain structures. It is constantly picking up information from our environment and sending it back to the brain for interpretation and action.

With signals consistently coming from our RAS in our lizard brain and the amygdala in the **limbic region**, our body and brain are at work 24/7 scanning the environment for clues and cues to determine whether or not we are safe. In social settings, this ongoing process of trying to sniff out danger has been called **neuroception**, our unconscious **safety-threat detection system** (Porges, 2011). This safety-threat detection system (Figure 3.4) works mainly through the body's **autonomic nervous system's** three major branches:

- *The parasympathetic nervous system.* It is focused on keeping us relaxed and seeks well-being by satisfying our needs for food, shelter, social relationships, and sex. It manages our relaxation response through easy breathing, a steady heartbeat, and the release of natural opioids such as **dopamine**, serotonin, and other endorphins.
- *The sympathetic nervous system.* This system is focused on keeping us alert and ready to react to avoid danger by fight, flight, or freeze. It prepares us for quick action by releasing adrenaline and cortisol to raise our heartbeat and prepare our muscles for a quick sprint.
- *The polyvagal nervous system.* It is our "social engagement system" and is focused on keeping us connected to others. Gopnik, Meltzoff, and Kuhl (2000) discovered that these nerves trigger our "contact urge," our desire to be with other people. All human beings have an innate contact urge. Collectivist cultural practices have reinforced this natural tendency and deepened the brain's hardwiring for relationships. This system encourages social bonding through the release of hormones such as **oxytocin** when we are in the presence of others. Social activities such as laughing, talking, and even hugging release oxytocin, the bonding hormone. When we feel safe in

the presence of another, our breath comes easily, our heartbeat is regulated, we don't sweat nervously, our thinking is clear, and we feel open, expansive, and in sync. Oxytocin is the brain's "stand down" signal to the amygdala.

In the previous section, we looked at how intellective capacity or brain-power is physically grown through the cellular structures in the brain. In this section, an important takeaway is that it's through the nervous system that individuals build the physical foundation for positive, receptive relationships. Relationships are not just emotional; they have a physical component. Relationships exist at the intersection of mind-body. They are the precursor to learning. When anyone experiences others in an environment like a class-room that is inattentive or hostile, the body picks up that information through the autonomic nervous system and sends it up to the RAS and amygdala. There the amygdala gets the information that it's not socially, emotionally, or intellectually safe and sends out a distress signal to the body. The body starts to produce stress hormones that make learning nearly impossible. Even if the environment isn't hostile but simply unwelcoming, the brain doesn't produce enough oxytocin and begins to experience anxiety. This anxiety triggers the sympathetic nervous system, making one think he is in danger because the brain doesn't experience a sense of community.

When we look at the stress some students experience in the classroom because they belong to marginalized communities because of race, class, language, or gender, we have to understand their safety-threat detection system is already cued to be on the alert for social and psychological threats based on past experience. It becomes imperative to understand how to build positive social relationships that signal to the brain a sense of physical, psychological, and social safety so that learning is possible.

Figure 3.4 Features of The Brain's Safety-Threat System

Systems	Avoiding	Approaching	Attaching
Purpose	Detect threats to physical, social, and psychological safety	Seek out well-being and reward despite obstacles	Connect with others in order to increase protection and connection
Brain Structures	Reticular Activating System (RAS), the amygdala, and the sympathetic nervous system	RAS, the thalamus, and the neocortex, and the parasympathetic nervous system	RAS and the polyvagal nervous system

(Continued)

Figure 3.4 (Continued)

Motto	Move Away From Pain	Move Toward Pleasure	Connect to Protect
Focus	Focused on assessing risk and threat in the environment based on deep culture and past experiences in sociopolitical context	Focus on increasing motivation to seek out those things that make one feel good physically, socially, and psychologically If something doesn't lead to reward, well-being or feeling good, the brain will not pursue it	Focus on finding a tribe to help share chores, find food, provide community so one can focus on learning, making art, reflection, exploration, and innovation
Physical Reactions	Release of cortisol, adrenaline to prepare for defense or escape when triggered Shrinks working memory	Release of dopamine to reward the effort of seeking well-being Motivates us to want to do it again	Release of oxytocin to encourage bonding with others The presence of oxytocin puts the safety-threat detection system in the amygdala on pause
Social Implications	Trust or lack of trust Self-protection over rapport	Engagement/ disengagement High or low self-motivation Growth or fixed mindset	Feeling included or marginalized Openness for connection or post traumatic stress Compassion or self-preservation

Source: Inspired by Hanson, R. (2013). *Hardwiring happiness: The new brain science of contentment, calm, and confidence.* New York: Harmony Books.

CULTURALLY RESPONSIVE BRAIN RULES

So, what do we do with all this information about the brain and how it works? I have integrated the most important information from the first three chapters into six core design principles to make it easier to remember and reference. When you understand these brain rules, it becomes easier to understand how the brain uses culture to interpret threats and opportunities. I have highlighted the implication each principle has on culturally responsive teaching.

Remember that no single principle stands alone. They all work together, but I've tried to tease them apart in order to highlight the unique qualities of each one. You will see these principles in later chapters along with details about how to operationalize them. The order of the principles isn't important, except for Number 1. It is always first.

1. *The brain seeks to minimize social threats and maximize opportunities to connect with others in community.*

The brain's two prime directives are to stay safe and be happy. The brain takes its social needs very seriously and is fierce in protecting an individual's sense of well-being, self-determination, and self-worth along with its connection to community. We cannot downplay students' need to feel safe and valued in the classroom. The brain will not seek to connect with others if it perceives them to be threatening to its social or psychological well-being based on what they say and do. It's important to point out that what a teacher may regard as an innocent gesture may be interpreted by the student as threatening. As a result, the amygdala stays on alert, trying to detect other **microaggressions**. Microaggressions are the subtle, everyday verbal and nonverbal slights, snubs, or insults which communicate hostile, derogatory, or negative messages to people of color based solely on their marginalized group membership. In many cases, these covert messages serve to invalidate positive group identity or trivialize their experiences. They are designed to demean them on a personal or group level, communicate they are lesser human beings, suggest they do not belong with the majority group, threaten and intimidate, or relegate them to inferior status and treatment (Sue et al., 2007).

As a culturally responsive teacher you have to familiarize yourself with common actions or conditions that make students feel unsafe, even if they cannot articulate this sense of threat. Your definition of what feels threatening or welcoming may be different from the students' definition. It is important to act according to students' definitions not your own.

In the end, dependent learners who don't feel supported are especially vulnerable to feeling threatened. This is our process of *neuroception*, the unconscious safety-threat detection system at work. They will avoid the perceived threat of public humiliation, going into fight, flight, or freeze mode.

It is not enough to have a classroom free of psychological and social threats. The brain needs to be part of a caring social community to maximize its sense of well-being. Marginalized students need to feel affirmed and included as valued members of a learning community.

2. Positive relationships keep our safety-threat detection system in check.

There is a reason that collectivist cultures focus on relationships. The brain is wired to scan continuously for social and physical threats, except when we are in positive relationships. The oxytocin positive relationships trigger helps the amygdala stay calm so the prefrontal cortex can focus on higher order thinking and learning. Just as you want to identify and remove things that create an emotionally unsafe environment, you have to also focus on building positive relationships that students recognize based on their cultural schema.

3. Culture guides how we process information.

Cultures with a strong oral tradition rely heavily on the brain's memory and social engagement systems to process new learning. Learning will be more effective if processed using the common cultural learning aids—stories, music, and repetition. These elements help build neural pathways and activate myelination. They help neurons fire and wire together in ways that make learning "sticky." Collectivist cultures use social interactions such as conversation and storytelling as learning aids. Because of society's history of segregation and unequal educational opportunities, many communities of color continue to use the natural learning modalities in the home and community. As a result, their neural pathways are primed to learn using story, art, movement, and music.

4. Attention drives learning.

Neuroscience reminds us that before we can be motivated to learn what is in front of us, we must pay attention to it. Every brain's RAS is tuned to novelty, relevance, and emotion, but each person interprets these three elements through his particular cultural lens. Cultures based on an oral tradition rely heavily on the RAS to activate learning, using music, call and response, and other attention grabbing strategies to signal something important. Learning isn't a passive event but a dynamic action. It requires focused attention, active engagement, and conscious processing by the learner. The hallmark of an independent learner is his ability to direct his attention toward his own learning.

5. All new information must be coupled with existing funds of knowledge in order to be learned.

Our limbic brain creates schema that operate as background knowledge. These internal scripts help us make sense of our external experiences. All learners have to connect new content to what they already know. What we already know is organized according to our cultural experiences, values, and concepts. For example, in Brazil, Paulo Freire taught reading skills by organizing his reading material around villagers' funds of knowledge. If they were farmers, he selected words and texts related to tools and processes related to farming. They already had deep neural pathways and complex schema around farming to connect the new written words to. Freire capitalized on the fact that their neurons around farming concepts, visual images, and now written words would all fire and wire together, strengthening their automaticity with decoding written words. So, to learn new content or skills, the brain figures out where to make connections to what we already know so that we "get it." To make learning stick, we have to determine what students already know and understand how they have organized it in their schema. From there we must construct culturally based connections or "scaffolds" between the existing schema and the new content.

6. *The brain physically grows through challenge and stretch, expanding its ability to do more complex thinking and learning.*

The brain's main purpose is to get smarter at surviving and thriving in life. Brain growth is stimulated when we have to figure out something new, engage in a complex task, or complete a puzzle. The brain's response is to literally grow more capacity in the form of neurons, dendrites, and synapses, topping it all off with a thick coat of myelin to increase speed. When we look at the educational experiences of many groups marginalized by race, language, or socioeconomics, we see that they often get a "watered down" curriculum that doesn't require higher order thinking. Consequently, they don't build the capacity to do higher order thinking on their own. To empower dependent learners and help them become independent learners, the brain needs to be challenged and stretched beyond its comfort zone with cognitive routines and strategy.

Culturally responsive teaching is also about empowerment and interrupting teaching practices that keep certain students dependent learners. We have to create the right instructional conditions that stimulate neuron growth and myelination by giving students work that is relevant and focused on problem solving. Just turning up the rigor of instruction or increasing the complexity of content will not stimulate brain growth. Instead, challenge and stretch come with learning the moves to do more strategic thinking and information processing.

IMPLICATIONS FOR SUPPORTING DEPENDENT LEARNERS AND BUILDING INTELLECTIVE CAPACITY

Dependent learners experience a great deal of stress and anxiety in the classroom as they struggle with certain learning tasks. This anxiety is amplified when they feel marginalized or unsupported because of their race, gender, or language. It is our responsibility to create the right conditions for optimum learning. We can only do that when we understand how the brain responds to threats—real or perceived. Our goal is to help culturally and linguistically diverse students easily reach a state of relaxed alertness—that combination of excitement and anticipation we call engagement—every day. As you design instruction and create classroom environments to authentically engage culturally and linguistically diverse students, keep in mind the brain rules. Authentic engagement begins with remembering that we are wired to connect with one another. In communal cultures, it is at the center of daily living and learning.

CHAPTER SUMMARY

- Building awareness as a culturally responsive teacher includes learning about how the brain physically works and its influence on our social-emotional state.
- The brain is guided by two interconnected prime directives: minimize threats and maximize well-being. Our culture and experiences within the sociopolitical context program our brains regarding how it interprets what is threatening and what is an opportunity for authentic connection with others.
- The first two layers of the brain play important roles in helping to detect and minimize social and physical threats, especially the amygdala. The third and newest layer, the neocortex, is where neuroplasticity takes place.
- We are hardwired to connect with others. Our nervous system is designed to guide us toward avoiding threats, approaching rewards and things that will make us feel good, and attaching to others for safety and companionship.
- Our challenge as culturally responsive teachers is knowing how to create an environment that the brain perceives as safe and nurturing so it can relax, let go of any stress, and turn its attention to learning.

INVITATION TO INQUIRY

- How do principles of neuroscience influence your teaching?
- What "brain rules" guide your lesson design?

GOING DEEPER

- *How the Brain Learns* (2011) by David A. Sousa
- *Soft-Wired: How the New Science of Brain Plasticity Can Change Your Life* (2013) by Dr. Michael Merzenich, PhD

4 Preparing to Be a Culturally Responsive Practitioner

The real voyage of discovery consists not in seeking new landscapes, but in having new eyes.

—Marcel Proust

When I dare to be powerful—to use my strength in the service of my vision, it becomes less and less important whether I am afraid.

—Audre Lorde, African American Poet

Up to this point our focus has been on understanding culture and brain structures as critical background knowledge. While we are still in the Awareness quadrant of the Ready for Rigor frame, I want to shift from thinking about the physical aspects of the brain and culture to a focus on emotional intelligence and implicit bias.

As I said earlier, culturally responsive teaching isn't a set of engagement strategies you use on students. Instead, think of it as a mindset, a way of looking at the world. Too often, we focus on only doing something to culturally and linguistically diverse students without changing ourselves, especially when our students are dependent learners who are not able to access their full academic potential on their own. Instead, culturally responsive teaching is about being a different type of teacher who is in relationship with students and the content in a different way. We will look at that new type of student-teacher relationship in the next chapter. In this chapter, we will explore how we can prepare ourselves to show up differently in our relationships with students.

Being responsive to diverse students' needs asks teachers to be mindful and present. That requires reflection. Engaging in reflection helps culturally responsive teachers recognize the beliefs, behaviors, and practices that get in the way of their ability to respond constructively and positively to students. The true power of culturally responsive teaching comes from being comfortable in your own skin because you are not a neutral party in the process. You can never take yourself out of the equation. Instead, you must commit to the journey. This means we each must do the "inside-out" work required: developing the right mindset, engaging in self-reflection, checking our implicit biases, practicing social-emotional awareness, and holding an inquiry stance regarding the impact of our interactions on students.

As a student, I had the privilege of having two highly skilled culturally responsive teachers. One was Mr. Ruane in tenth grade. He was a White teacher who coached football and taught African American literature. What I remember most about him was how comfortable he was talking about issues of race, culture, and society in a room full of African American kids who took his elective class at the height of the Black Power movement. He wasn't scared or overwhelmed by our teenaged outrage at "the Man" and bold self-expression with giant Afros and raised fists. It never seemed to make him nervous. Instead, he was able to harness that energy in service of teaching us analytical literacy skills and the love of poetry as a form of self-expression. In retrospect, I can see how he used the poetry to cultivate our academic mindset. I can still remember the class discussion around Paul Laurence Dunbar's (1997) poem, *We Wear the Mask*, that he offered up as a life compass and opportunity to shape our own identities as learners. Some of my greatest life lessons came from what I learned in his classroom. And it wasn't just his instructional technique. He made me feel seen, heard, and cared for as a learner. I believe Mr. Ruane was able to support us because he was comfortable in his own cultural skin. He didn't try to be hip or "down" with us. Whatever his implicit biases might have been, he managed them internally and didn't allow them to direct how he responded to us.

As we walk through this chapter, I want to offer strategies and tools for preparing yourself to be an emotionally conscious culturally responsive educator. Before you can leverage diversity as an asset in the classroom, you must reflect on the challenges that can interfere with open acceptance of students who are different from you in background, race, class, language, or gender.

UNPACKING OUR IMPLICIT BIAS

The philosopher Lao Tzu said that the journey of a thousand miles begins with the first step, and becoming an effective culturally responsive teacher is a long journey. One challenge is learning how to access and shift your implicit biases. As we do, we have to learn to navigate around the lizards in the road. I am not referring to actual lizards but instead to that internal gatekeeper known as our lizard brain that we talked about in Chapter 3. As you begin your own inside-out work in this area, your lizard brain will start to freak out. It's afraid that you will have to talk about sensitive issues such as race, racism, classism, sexism, or any other kind of "-ism." It is afraid that this conversation will make you vulnerable and open to some type of emotional or physical attack. But this fear is not real. It is just your amygdala's ploy to get you to stay in your comfort zone.

Remember, the lizard brain ruled by the amygdala and reticular activating system (RAS), is designed to keep us safe. It thinks that the safest place for us is deep in the center of our comfort zone surrounded by the moat of our unconscious, implicit biases. When we venture too close to the edges of our comfort zone, it sounds an alarm designed to remind us of the dangers that exist outside. Your lizard brain will try a variety of scare tactics. Physically, it will flood your brain with stress hormones such as cortisol and adrenaline to short circuit your more rational thought processes as you step outside your comfort zone or it will put you in freeze, fight, or flight mode. It will try to keep you in check with narratives such as "you need to be color-blind, not calling attention to racial, cultural, or language differences" or "we are all the same inside. Skin color doesn't matter anymore." You might experience impatience with the process as your lizard brain tells you, "This isn't for me. I am a person of color so I already know this" or "this is for White folks." It might even tell you lies such as "I don't have a culture so this is just a waste of time," "They are going to call you a racist if you bring this stuff up," or "This is just touchy-feely crap."

Take a step back and recognize what is going on. This is why understanding social neuroscience—how the brain responds and interacts with others—is critical to a culturally responsive practitioner. There is no way to dismantle implicit bias without controlling this first stage of the process. Instead, accept the challenge of venturing into the unknown with an open mind and heart. Our lizard brain doesn't respond to rationality or language. It is wired only for pure emotion and feeling. Neuropsychologist Rick Hanson, author of *Hardwiring Happiness* says that the key strategy to calming the lizard brain is to practice relaxation and mindfulness. So, start a meditation practice, take up yoga, or join a drumming circle. Spend time in nature. Research in neurobiology proves that these techniques reduce the fight or flight hormones that get released when our brains feel a physical or social threat. This might seem like an odd suggestion in a book about culturally responsive teaching but it is actually in keeping with the cultural practices of collectivist cultures—spending time in nature keeps us grounded and centered during challenging times. It is part of our resilience strategy.

Begin With an Intention

Intention is the starting point for preparing yourself for improving your culturally responsive teaching practice. The act of committing to the process primes your brain and activates your will. The commitment to be an effective educator of culturally diverse dependent learners builds the stamina and courage to persevere when the process gets challenging. To make the path feel less uncharted, find real and virtual mentors who have already walked the path. Find someone of a similar racial, cultural or class background so that you can see how she developed her practice. Read about the journey of White writing teacher and social justice advocate, Linda Christensen, woven throughout her books *Reading, Writing, and Rising Up* (2000) or *Teaching for Joy and Justice* (2009). Seek out Tim Wise, author of *White Like Me: Reflections on Race from a Privileged Son* (2011) or African American educator, bell hooks (1994) in her collection of essays in *Teaching to Transgress*. Math educator Bob Moses, founder of the Algebra Project, shares some of his journey in *Radical Equations* (2002). Read about the lessons learned from the year-long, cross-cultural teaching inquiry conducted by Jennifer Obidah and Karen Teel in *Because of the Kids: Facing Racial and Cultural Differences in Schools* (2001).

Self-Examination: Making the Familiar Strange

The next stage is to examine your own cultural identity. Culture is like the air we breathe, permeating all we do. And the hardest culture to examine is often our own, because it shapes our actions in ways that seem invisible and normal. What feels "normal," Small (1998) reminds us, is molded by deeply ingrained social habits and ways of valuing and evaluating what we are scarcely aware of. This is what implicit bias is in a nutshell.

Learning about one's own culture—or "making the familiar strange" as anthropologist George Spindler calls it—is far more challenging than learning about the culture of others ("making the strange familiar") (Spindler & Spindler, 1982). A critical first step for teachers is to understand how their own cultural values shape their expectations in the classroom—from how they expect children to behave socially, take turns during discussions, or even pass out classroom materials. A student's different way of being or doing can be perceived as a deviation from the norm and therefore problematic if we don't recognize that it is just different. This might not be an issue in our day-to-day lives, but when we are the authority figure in the classroom, we have the power to penalize those students who seem to be acting in ways that are inconsistent with our cultural view.

Culturally responsive teaching calls for teachers to take the "emotional risk" to examine the deeply held beliefs that influence how they respond to students. This inward reflection means being willing to listen and change in order to respond positively and constructively to the student who may be culturally different in some way. We have to confront our discomfort through self-reflection and analysis of our underlying assumptions in order to become aware of the unconscious biases that influence our teaching.

Here are three internal tasks every teacher has to work through to uncover implicit bias and prepare to work with culturally and linguistically diverse students. We will look at each in depth:

1. Identify your cultural frame of reference

2. Widen your cultural aperture

3. Identify your key triggers

Identify Your Cultural Frames of Reference

The first step in making the familiar strange is to take an inquiry stance toward the examination of your cultural identity. We usually ask teachers to investigate aspects of their cultural identity *after* they have encountered cultural conflict in the classroom, which is often too late (Delpit, 1995). In reality, if teachers want to be successful in their work with culturally diverse students, they must first accept and understand themselves as cultural beings (Marshall, 2002). This self-knowledge acts as a set of reference points that shape our mental models about teaching, learning, and dependent learners of color.

Map Your Cultural Reference Points

Create time and space to work your way through aspects of surface, shallow, and deep culture for clues about your own culture. Think of it as a treasure hunt or an archeological dig. Set time aside to journal and do inquiry around key questions. Don't try to answer these questions in one sitting. Instead, plan to sit with the questions before trying to answer them. This gives your brain time to sift through memories. Pull out some old photo albums or diaries as a trigger. If you can, do some interviews about family cultural practices or views.

Think about your surface culture:

- How did your family identify ethnically or racially?
- Where did you live—urban, suburban, or rural community?
- What is the story of your family in America? Has your family been here for generations, a few decades, or just a few years?
- How would you describe your family's economic status—middle class, upper class, working class, or low income? What did that mean in terms of quality of life?
- Were you the first in your family to attend college? If not, who did— your parents, grandparents, or great-grandparents?
- What family folklore or stories did you regularly hear growing up?
- What are some of your family traditions—holidays, foods, or rituals?
- Who were the heroes celebrated in your family and/or community? Why? Who were the antiheroes? Who were the "bad guys"?

Spend some time sifting through your shallow cultural beliefs and experiences with these questions:

- What metaphors, analogies, parables, or "witty" sayings do you remember hearing from parents, grandparents, aunts, and uncles?
- What family stories are regularly told or referenced? What message do they communicate about core values?
- Review primary messages from your upbringing: What did your parents, neighbors, and other authority figures tell you respect looked like? Disrespect?
- How were you trained to respond to different emotional displays— crying, anger, and happiness?
- What physical, social, or cultural attributes were praised in your community? Which ones were you taught to avoid?
- How were you expected to interact with authority figures? Was authority of teachers and other elders assumed or did it have to be earned?
- As a child, did you call adults by their first name?
- What got you shunned or shamed in your family?
- What earned you praise as a child?
- Were you allowed to question, or talk back to, adults? Was it okay to call adults by their first name?
- What's your family/community's relationship with time?

Now, do a similar reflection on your deep cultural values related to communication, "doing school," self-motivation, and effort. List those learning behaviors you believe every student should exhibit—talk and discourse patterns, volume of interaction, time on task, collaboration or individual work, seat time versus interaction. Ask yourself how did you come to believe this? What messages did you get about why other racial or ethnic groups succeeded or not? What did your culture teach you about intelligence? Did you grow up believing it was set at birth? Did you believe it was genetic? Did you believe some groups were smarter than others?

As you develop a greater sense of your cultural frames of reference, you should begin to have a clearer picture of your cultural self—what drives you, what shapes your worldview, and what influences your teaching. You will begin to get a glimpse of your implicit biases throughout the process.

Widen Your Interpretation Aperture

We all operate from a set of cultural frames of reference. The challenge is that if we routinely interpret other people's actions solely through our personal cultural frames, we run the risk of misinterpreting their actions or intentions.

When I am talking with teachers about this idea of interpreting other's behavior through our own cultural frame of reference, I use the example of an exchange between an African American student and a White teacher that Lisa Delpit highlights in her seminal piece, "The Silenced Dialogue" (1988). The student was up and out of his seat sharpening his pencil along with other students as the teacher was about to begin the lesson. She got his attention and said, "James, would you like to take your seat?" James said no and continued to sharpen his pencil. The teacher became outraged and sent James to the principal's office for being defiant. James was surprised and didn't understand why he was being sent to the office. When asked what happened, he said the teacher asked him a question and he answered her question.

This exchange highlights classic cross-cultural miscommunication (Dray & Wisneski, 2011). In reality, the teacher was not asking James a question or giving him a choice. Indirect directives are a feature of White middle class cultural communication style. At home and in his community, James recognized someone giving him a directive because it was direct—"James, take your seat, please" rather than posed as a question with choices. The teacher assumed that James knew she was giving him a directive, and he was consciously refusing to obey it. She interpreted his response as evidence of his intention to be defiant and oppositional.

Create Space for Alternative Explanations

Many teachers don't always think about the cultural lens that influences their interpretations of student actions, parent responses, or their own instructional styles. Instead, we fall back on our default programming, which leads often to deficit thinking.

Figure 4.1 What Is the Deficit Thinking Paradigm?

When operating from a deficit thinking paradigm, educators and policymakers believe that culturally and linguistically diverse students fail in school because of their own deficiencies or because their families don't value education, not because of social inequities, unfair school policies, or differential treatment in the classroom. There is an ill-informed belief that a student's failures are attributable to the student's lack of intellectual ability, linguistic inferiority, or family dysfunction. This deficit perspective suggests that efforts to improve academic achievement should be focused on "fixing" students (i.e., improving test-taking skills) rather than shifting the school culture to support intellective capacity building and identity-safe classrooms so that students can access their academic potential. As a result, teachers' deficit-oriented attributions of student performance influence their instructional decision making, resulting in giving students less opportunity for engaging curricula, interesting tasks, and culturally congruent ways of learning.

The solution is to broaden our body of explanations and interpretations of student actions. We usually talk about sharpening our "cultural lens" as culturally responsive teachers. Rather than using the metaphor of a lens, I want to offer the metaphor of an aperture. An aperture is a hole or an opening through which light travels. The word aperture shows up in both optics and photography. Our natural aperture is found in our eyes. The pupil, our eye's aperture, opens and closes to let in more light so that we are able to see more clearly under certain conditions. In photography, the camera's aperture lets in more or less light so that the picture comes out clear and bright enough. In a similar way, we have to let in more alternative explanations for students' learning behaviors and social interactions that look different from our own. Otherwise, we run the risk of misinterpreting students' learning behaviors as intellectual deficits.

So we have to develop a process that allows us to expand our ability to recognize the different ways things are done in other cultures. Cross-cultural communication experts, Gudykunst and Kim (2003) offer a three-part process for widening our interpretative aperture that can serve as an internal protocol—*description, interpretation,* and *evaluation.* Let's imagine we are watching two fourth-grade Latina girls doing an assignment at their desks, which are organized in quads. You look over and see them talking back and forth, not in loud, disruptive voices, but low murmuring. One of the girls begins to write on her paper. Then they begin talking again. What is going on?

- **Description**—The first step is to simply describe what you see. The girls are talking. Then they are writing and then resume talking. Leave out any interpretation or judgment of the action. Just include observable phenomenon. What did the person say or do? How did the event unfold? Our own implicit biases will want to jump in to interpret or judge the behavior or interaction.
- **Interpretation**—The next step involves interpreting what is going on. To interpret something, you have to give it meaning. So let's go back to our two girls. They are talking and then writing when each is supposed to be doing her own work. You may interpret their talking as cheating. Or you might consider another interpretation of their behavior. You can see it as a culturally grounded collaborative learning behavior. You see it as instructional conversation that is helping them each process the task and come to their own conclusions. Each interpretation carries with it implications for being or not being culturally responsive.
- **Evaluation**—The last step in the process involves assigning positive or negative significance to the action based on our initial interpretation. If we interpreted their talking and writing as cheating, then we judge them as untrustworthy, not smart because they couldn't do the work on their own, or lazy. Our interaction with those two girls would be negative based on how we chose to interpret and judge their behavior. If we decided to interpret it as collaboration and instructional conversation, we might judge them as resourceful, acting like they belong to a community of learners.

The first part of the process, description, is inherently neutral in terms of meaning. Think of what you would see if a video camera recorded an event or interaction. Usually, given the fast pace of the classroom, as teachers we have a tendency to move quickly through description into interpretation. Even then we usually offer only one interpretation of the student's behavior or motivations and that's often from our own perspective. Most culturally responsive teachers recognize the need to develop their observation skills so they can effectively describe what is happening during an interaction with a student or when watching a scenario play out between students and not jump to conclusions. This allows the time and space to entertain alternative explanations. Over time, your interpretation aperture expands.

There's a word of caution here. When students are behaving badly, hurting themselves or others, or disrupting the learning environment, we cannot ignore that and chalk it up to "that's how they do it in their culture." Professor and culturally responsive pedagogy expert Sharroky Hollie reminds us that we also have to recognize "situational appropriateness," meaning that a student's actions may represent positive cultural behavior but may not be appropriate for the situation. A student's behavior might not even be acceptable in his own culture. I always check by asking, *"Do you do that in front of your grandmother?"* As our interpretation aperture expands, we can help students consciously select culturally different ways of speaking or interacting that are still appropriate to the situation.

Here are tips to help you use the Mindful Reflection protocol as a reflection tool:

1. ***Spend some time viewing the replay in your mind***. Try to review what happened without judgment. Describe it almost like stage directions. For example, here's what we see when we review the replay of the interaction with James. James walked to the pencil sharpener. Seven other children were up and out of their seats. The teacher moved to the front of the room. She spoke to two other students before she spoke to James. She asked James a question. James responded to the question in a neutral tone of voice and continued to sharpen his pencil. Once he finished, he turned to return to his seat. As he walked to his seat, the teacher told him to go to the principal's office.

2. ***Make a list of your assumptions, reactions, and interpretations of behaviors as the scenario replays***. What specific thing did you react to? How did you interpret it? Based on what belief or assumption?

   In the James scenario, the teacher reacted to James' answer to her question. Her assumption was that James knew that even though she was stating her request as a question with choices, she was actually giving him a direct order. She interpreted his answer as being intentionally defiant. She evaluated his behavior as negative.

3. ***Try on alternative explanations***. Select one or two student reactions or interactions (what he said or did) and try to offer alternative explanations for the student's behavior based on what you are learning about his deep cultural beliefs, norms, or practices. In the

James scenario, the teacher might revisit James' response to her directive since that is what she reacted to. She might reflect on what she is learning about cultural communication patterns (part of one's shallow culture). She might start with doing some inquiry around communication styles. In James' home culture, how are directives given? What is considered an appropriate or inappropriate response? These would be the questions she pays attention to as she continues her virtual immersion in James' culture.

4. ***Check your explanations***. Share your alternative explanations with other culturally responsive teachers in your professional learning community or those in your own personal learning circle. Talk with cultural informants who can give you insight into the positive expression of cultural beliefs and norms. James' teacher could write this interaction up as a critical incident and share it with others to get more input and insight.

5. ***Build your cross-cultural background knowledge***. Recognize that understanding alternative explanations for student behavior is an ongoing process. There is no list to study or Wikipedia page to search online. To be a culturally responsive teacher means committing to being a lifelong learner. Widen your interpretation aperture by exposing yourself to other cultural experiences similar to those of the students you serve so you can experience alternative ways of doing and being.

6. ***Leverage technology and watch positive movies or television series that will allow you to virtually step into another cultural experience***. Ask for recommendations. There are movies, documentaries, and television series about a variety of cultural experiences—racial, geographical, gender, or language. Watch (don't judge) and study communication styles, nonverbal communication cues and gestures, or how core values are expressed in daily life. Begin to see the patterns that cut across the cultural archetypes of individualism and collectivism as explained in Chapter 2, also look for variations within a particular archetype that cut across race and class. For example, both African American and Latino cultures are very communal, but each culture situates individual recognition and standing out differently.

Identify Your Triggers

Communicating across cultures opens up the potential for miscommunication and unintended conflict. When we try to manage and

| **Figure 4.2** | Mindful Reflection Protocol by Dray & Wisneski |

Step 1:	**Explain the attributions that you have about the student.**
	a. Describe what you and the student said and did.
	b. How did the student react to your actions or comments?
	c. Collect notes on multiple days and at different times of the day.
Step 2:	**Write out or reflect on your feelings and thoughts when working with the student. Take into account the potential for misinterpretations resulting from deficit thinking, prejudice, and overgeneralizations.**
	a. How does this student make you feel? What are your worries or fears?
	b. What are your assumptions? Why do you find the student problematic?
	c. Have you evaluated, interpreted, or described the behavior?
	d. Try to rewrite the examples in descriptive terms.
Step 3:	**Consider alternative explanations by reviewing your documentation and reflections.**
	a. Review the explanations and reflect on why the student may be doing what he or she does. Look for patterns in your behavior and the student's behavior.
	b. What are your expectations for the situation? How is the student not meeting your expectations? In what way is the behavior interfering with learning?
	c. List alternative explanations or interpretations of the student's behavior.
	d. What external factors and/or personal factors could be influencing the student's behavior? What recent changes have occurred in the student's life, disability, acculturation, and so forth?
Step 4:	**Check your assumptions. Share your reflections with a colleague, parents, and/or community members. Meet with parents to learn more about expected and observed behaviors in the home.**
	a. Share your list of alternative explanations or interpretations of the student's behavior with a colleague, parents, and/or community members.
	b. Meet with the family to learn more about their perspective in understanding the behavior. Do they notice the same behavior at home? Do they find it problematic? How do they interact with the student at home? Have there been any major changes or upsets in the home?
	c. Be open and responsive to the family's ideas and perspectives. Seek to understand rather than to judge.

(Continued)

| Figure 4.2 | (Continued) |

Step 5:	Make a plan.
	a. How will you change or respond differently?
	b. Brainstorm ideas on how to change the environment, your actions, and/or expectations for this student.
	c. Experiment with responding differently. Note what happens. Reflect on your feelings as well as the student's response.
	d. Frequently communicate with the family. Ask whether family members have noticed a difference. What have they been trying that works?
	e. Consult with colleagues, parents, and/or community members while you experiment to check your assumptions and interpretations.
Step 6:	**Continuously revisit this process to reassess your attributions and your progress with the student.**
	a. Notice when you are overgeneralizing, attributing behavior within a deficit perspective, or behaving in prejudiced ways toward certain students.
	b. Remember that this process is a continuous one, so revisit the steps periodically to continue your growth and understanding of students.

Source: B. Dray & D. Wisneski in Mindful Reflection as a Process for Developing Culturally Responsive Practices. *TEACHING Exceptional Children*, Sept-Oct 2011.

navigate across cultural differences, our brain is on the lookout for signs of danger or signs of well-being based on our cultural frames of reference. When we feel a threat of any sort—including threats to our belief systems—we are vulnerable to an amygdala hijack. Remember your RAS acts like the brain's emotional "smoke detector," always scanning for things that might cause social embarrassment or emotional pain when we are communicating cross-culturally, ready to sound the alarm that jolts us into fight and flight mode. *When our brain's alarm system gets triggered, we become culturally reactive in an effort to protect ourself rather than culturally responsive to the other person we are interacting with.*

We all get hijacked at times, but culturally responsive teachers know themselves well enough to anticipate situations that might trigger them. They have tools and techniques to avoid or short-circuit an amygdala overreaction. A key readiness skill or capacity the culturally responsive teacher develops is the ability to manage her emotions and reframe potential threats. To reduce the possibility of getting hijacked, it is important to practice mental strategies and physical tools to prevent or de-escalate the amygdala's reaction. The culturally responsive teacher's ability to manage her emotions is paramount because she is the "emotional thermostat" of the classroom and can influence students' mood and productivity.

Recognizing Common Triggers

An important part of identifying your triggers is recognizing universal triggers that are hardwired into the brain. The field of social neuroscience has identified some of the high alert categories that have been hardwired into our amygdala. Think of it as preloaded software that every person comes with as a result of human development over time. Research has shown that humans have a fundamental need to belong, are incredibly sensitive to their social context, and are strongly motivated to remain in good standing with their social group to avoid social exclusion (Rock, 2009).

There are five elements of social interaction that activate strong threats and rewards in the brain, thus influencing how we react in given situations: *standing, certainty, connection, control, and equity* (Figure 4.3). They have a strong influence on our implicit bias and cultural frames of reference. Do some reflection and think about which ones trigger you.

Figure 4.3 Social Interaction Elements That Activate Threats in the Brain

Element	Description	What's the Threat
Standing	Standing refers to one's sense of importance relative to others in one's social network or organizational hierarchy (e.g., peers, coworkers, friends, supervisors). It also relates to how one believes others in the group perceive him—negative or positive, competent or incompetent.	The fear that one would be expelled from the "tribe" (such as being fired from a job, evaluated poorly by the principal, ostracized by peers because of doing things differently).
Certainty	Certainty refers to one's need for clarity and predictability in a social situation in order to make accurate social moves. It also relates to one's ability to predict what will happen (e.g., routines, cause and effect, action and reaction).	The fear of possibly embarrassing oneself or being unable to know what to do in a given situation. The feelings of being out of control or unable to be safe because of venturing into the unknown with new teaching practices and unfamiliar ways of organizing the classroom.

(Continued)

Figure 4.3 (Continued)

Element	Description	What's the Threat
Control	Control speaks to one's sense of control over his life and the perception that one's behavior can have a positive effect on the outcome of a situation (e.g., getting a promotion, finding a partner) rather than something out of his control having more influence (e.g., class, race, language, or gender).	The fear of someone telling you what to do, where to go, and how to behave that is inconsistent with your values (such as with English only laws or Jim Crow laws).
Connection	Relatedness focuses on one's sense of connection to and security with another person, one's family, or one's peer group. It also is concerned with whether new people one interacts with are friend or foe.	The fear of being an outsider and excluded. We fear losing important connection with others. People do not want to be out of relationship with others, especially an important peer group.
Equity	Equity refers to having a sense of fair, just, and nonbiased exchange between people (e.g., equal opportunity, equivalent pay for equivalent work, the elimination of unearned advantage and disadvantage).	The threat can come when one feels he or his group (class, geographic, linguistic) is being subjected to unearned disadvantage or someone is receiving unearned advantage. It may also be associated with distancing oneself from unearned advantage.

Practicing Emotional Self-Management

Self-management involves being aware of one's feelings and the ability to use this awareness as information to manage and adjust one's emotional state. For a culturally responsive teacher who is working to empower dependent learners who may be resistant out of fear, this practice is critical.

From neuroscience, we know emotions are contagious, so if one person in the classroom gets emotionally hijacked, it's likely others will be infected with anxiety, resistance, or disengagement. So just as we take precautions not to spread physical viruses, we want to avoid spreading toxic emotions that make everyone reactive rather than responsive. Remember that the brain has a **negativity bias**, meaning that the brain is more than 20 times more focused on negative experiences than on positive ones. Think Velcro versus Teflon. There are steps you can take to calm your amygdala.

Identify what sets you off. Think about which of the five areas of social threat make you defensive—class issues, geographic/regional differences, racial differences? Sometimes we know in advance that we're going to be in a conversation or a situation that is likely to set us off. In those cases, it's a good idea to take some time in advance to ask yourself: "What am I trying to do in this situation and how do I need to show up to make that outcome likely? How do I want to respond when that person does something that pushes my anger button?" By thinking it through in advance you're using your prefrontal cortex and are programming it to help keep your amygdala in check.

Label your feelings when they come up. For decades, psychologists, counselors, priests, and educators have been helping people identify or label their feelings. Now we know from new research using functional MRI imaging of the brain that labeling these feelings helps reduce their intensity and return some of the activity back to the prefrontal cortex along with more cognitive control. They call it "affect labeling." This process helps you cognitively reappraise or reframe negative feelings, thereby reducing their impact.

Begin by stating what's happening: If you can either say out loud or to yourself, "I'm getting angry here," you put yourself in the role of observer rather than actor. It is easier to make thoughtful choices about what to do next if you can decouple yourself from being the actor.

Create an "early warning system." Knowing what causes an amygdala hijack can help you head it off. By paying attention to signs and emotions you can take action early rather than allowing the amygdala to completely take over. *Notice your physical reaction.* When threatened or angered, most people have physical cues that they're headed down that path. It could be a tightening of your jaw, a flush feeling in your face, your vocal cords tightening up or something else. If you notice that, it's a cue to step back and regroup.

The S.O.D.A. Strategy

Here S.O.D.A. is not a carbonated drink, but a strategy for gaining control of our emotions when we feel triggered or our buttons have been pushed. S.O.D.A. is an acronym that stands for Stop, Observe, Detach and Awaken. The strategy is based on neuroscience findings that tell us that if we are able to put as little as 10 seconds in-between the time we get triggered and our reaction, we can preempt an amygdala hijack and avoid responding negatively. The following box gives an overview of the S.O.D.A. strategy.

Stop. This first step simply asks you to stop and pause rather than react in habitual ways. When you enter an interaction that feels challenging, work hard to stay open-minded. Open-mindedness means being open to other points of view, other ways of doing things, and staying open to changing your own view point. This might mean not allowing a certain cultural display such as a student's animated verbal exchange trigger you.

Observe. In the second step, check yourself. Don't react to what is going on. Instead, take a breath. Use the 10-second rule. When the brain gets triggered, it takes stress hormones approximately 10 seconds to move through the body to the prefrontal cortex. In the pre-hijack stage, the biochemicals cortisol and adrenaline are just beginning to kick in. There is still some "wiggle room" to listen to your wiser self and begin using stress management techniques to interrupt the amygdala takeover effectively. Try to describe to yourself what is happening in neutral terms. It is during this step that you can recognize that what was originally perceived as a threat isn't really.

Detach. Sometimes when we get triggered, we get personally invested in being right or exercising our power over others. Deliberately shift your consciousness to more pleasant or inspirational images. If those techniques fail, go get a drink of water, literally take a few steps back to shake yourself up a bit. When we can detach from the goal of being right or defending ourselves, we can redirect our energy toward being more responsive rather than reactive.

Awaken. When our amygdala reacts, it's because we are trying to protect ourselves. Shifting focus from yourself to the other person in front of you helps you "wake up" or become present in the moment. Try to see the other person as someone with his own feelings. He might be scared and reacting out of fear. Ask yourself a few questions about the other person. What are they thinking? How are they feeling in this moment? Shifting over to their perspective will get you out of your own reactive mode and will put you in a better position to have a positive interaction.

IMPLICATIONS FOR SUPPORTING DEPENDENT LEARNERS AND BUILDING INTELLECTIVE CAPACITY

In this chapter, we looked at three key areas of prep work to get yourself ready to be a culturally responsive teacher or to take your practice to the next level. Think about how you will organize yourself to move the work forward. Don't be overwhelmed by thinking you have to master each area before you can consider yourself competent. Find one or two high-leverage activities in each area and work on them for a specific time period. Structure life so that you have protected time for the type of internal excavation this requires. For example, use the six-week grading period to focus exclusively on doing inquiry around widening your interpretation of student behaviors. Maybe a few hours every Sunday can be devoted toward the more personal cultural identity work. Find other colleagues for accountability and support.

The old adage we usually hear is that "practice makes perfect." Based on what we know about neuroplasticity and deliberate practice, we should rephrase that to read, "practice makes permanent." As you organize yourself for this self-reflective prep work, remember that it is not about being perfect but about creating new neural pathways that shift your default cultural programming as you grow in awareness and skill.

CHAPTER SUMMARY

- Culturally responsive teachers have to understand their own cultural reference points to be effective.
- They must practice self-management to maintain their emotional intelligence and grow their cultural I.Q.
- Culturally responsive teachers learn to expand their interpretations of student behavior to include different cultural displays of learning and social interaction.

INVITATION TO INQUIRY

- What are your current cultural frames of reference?
- What processes have you engaged in to examine your own deep culture?
- What student social and learning behaviors trigger you in the classroom?
- What bias or assumptions might be behind your triggers?
- How do you manage your emotional intelligence in cross-cultural interactions?

GOING DEEPER

- *Because of the Kids: Facing Racial and Cultural Differences in Schools* (2001) by Jennifer Obidah and Karen Teel
- *Everyday Anti-Racism: Getting Real About Race in School* (2008) edited by Mica Pollack
- *Colormute: Race Talk Dilemmas in an American School* (2005) by Mica Pollack

PART II

Building Learning Partnerships

5 Building the Foundation of Learning Partnerships

Beginning with Meaningful Relationships

The best teachers teach from the heart, not the book.

—Horace Mann, American Educator

I've learned that people will forget what you said, people will forget what you did, but people will never forget how you made them feel.

—Maya Angelou

We laid the foundations for building a practice around self-awareness in the last chapter. Now we turn our attention to the students, the classroom, and the content. Too often though, we ignore the quality of our interactions with students and instead focus primarily on the curriculum. In culturally responsive teaching, relationships are as important as the curriculum. Geneva Gay, pioneer of culturally responsive pedagogy (2010) says positive relationships exemplified as "caring" are one of the major pillars of culturally responsive teaching. This reality stands in contrast to the dominant factory model of schooling, with its focus on the technical aspects of curriculum coverage and testing to sort and label students. In the factory model, relationship building is seen as a secondary issue related to class-room management more than to learning. The second practice area of the Ready for Rigor frame is focused on reframing and repositioning student-teacher relationships as the key ingredient in helping culturally and linguistically diverse dependent learners authentically engage. Even for high achieving students of color, positive relationships help them reach their fullest potential under less stress.

Why? In a collectivist, community-based culture, relationships are the foundation of all social, political, and cognitive endeavors. This is consistent with the fact that all human beings are hardwired for relationships after living in communal, cooperative settings for millions of years. Back when early man roamed the savannah populated with wild animals, living in community offered protection from these physical threats as well as from attack by hostile neighbors. Maintaining healthy relationships became very important so one wasn't ejected from the protection of the village. As pointed out in Chapter 2, relationships became so important to well-being and safety that the brain created an entire social engagement system to ensure we stay connected and in good standing with the tribe (Porges, 2011).

At the core of positive relationships is trust. Caring is the way that we generate the trust that builds relationships. We have to not only care *about* students in a general sense but also actively care *for* them in a physical and emotional sense. Cammarota and Romero (2006) highlight in their research, *A Critically Compassionate Intellectualism for Latino/a Students: Raising Voices Above the Silencing in Our Schools*, that many teachers and students at all grade levels report feeling disconnected from each other and, at times, even distrustful of one another. This is especially true when building relationships across racial, ethnic, and socioeconomic lines where implicit bias can get in the way (Howard, 2002; Quiroz, 2001). Stephen Brookfield, author of *The Skillful Teacher* (2000) calls relationships the "affective glue" in teaching and learning:

> Trust between teachers and students is the affective glue that binds educational relationships together. Not trusting teachers has several consequences for students. They are unwilling to submit themselves to the perilous uncertainties of new learning. They avoid risk. They keep their most deeply felt concerns private. They view with cynical reserve the exhortations and instructions of teachers. (p. 162)

Neuroscience tells us the brain feels safest and relaxed when we are connected to others we trust to treat us well. It responds to this sense of connection by secreting oxytocin, called the bonding hormone. Oxytocin makes us want to build a trusting relationship with the other person we are interacting with. Simple gestures, a smile, simple nod of the head, a pat on the back, or touch of the arm from another person stimulates the release of oxytocin in the recipient. I know a White school leader of a unique charter elementary school serving Cambodian, Latino, and African American students who acknowledges each student she passed in the hall with a simple greeting and what I called her "Namaste" pause. She would pause slightly and turn her attention to the student and give an almost imperceptible bow in the student's direction. Every time, I witness the students' faces lighting up at this small gesture of **affirmation** and respect.

Ironically, researchers found that when participants in one study felt they had won the trust of another, their own brains responded by producing oxytocin. Being seen as trustworthy by another stimulates the brain for connection. To make sure we connect with others, our brains developed *mirror neurons* to keep us in sync with each other. Mirror neurons are special brain cells that prompt us to mimic others. Observing another person engaged in a particular behavior will light up regions in our brains as if we were actually doing it too. These special brain cells prompt us to mimic or "mirror" the behavior. It's the reason why when someone we are talking with smiles, we also smile. They cross their legs, we cross our legs. Mirror neurons encourage us to match our body language and facial expressions to the other person's to signal trust and rapport. Our neuroception kicks in to help us read the situation. This synchronizing dance triggers our relaxation response, and we feel more trusting. This is more than neuroscientific trivia. The culturally responsive teacher uses this information to make a more personal and authentic connection with students across differences.

THE NEED FOR A DIFFERENT KIND OF RELATIONSHIP

When I was in elementary school, my teachers would describe me as "a handful." I was always talking to other kids at the wrong time, talking back to the teacher, and generally off task. This went on from second grade until I met my match in fourth grade with Mrs. Morris. Rather than put up with my shenanigans, send me out of the classroom, or put me down with sarcastic remarks as some of my other teachers had, she took a different approach. She'd give me that look that said you know better. Other times, I realized she was actually studying me when she was looking in my direction. She initiated a different type of relationship with me that forced me, as a 9-year-old, to rethink my behavior and my own identity as a learner.

During my early days as a teacher when I thought about Mrs. Morris, I realized that culturally responsive relationships aren't just something nice to have. They are critical. The only way to get students to open up to us is to show we authentically care about who they are, what they have to say, and how they feel. Building a culture of care that helps dependent learners move toward independence requires what I call a **learning partnership**. Gay (2010) points out that caring within a culturally responsive context automatically places teachers in a different kind of emotional and academic partnership with students. This relationship is anchored in affirmation, mutual respect, and **validation** that breeds an unshakable belief that marginalized students not only *can* but *will* improve their school achievement (p. 52). The learning partnership is made up of three components that work together to turn this unshakable belief into reality. Think of it as an equation: **rapport** + **alliance** = **cognitive insight**. Each part of the learning partnership is essential. You can't ignore one and expect to develop the others.

Each phase acts as a stepping-stone to the next. First, building rapport focuses on establishing an emotional connection and building trust. In the alliance phase, we use this emotional connection to create a partnership that has the teacher and student coming together as a team to tackle a specific learning challenge. Each agrees to bring their will and skill to the effort. Because there's trust, the teacher can provide a degree of "push" or challenge without having the student experience an "amygdala hijack" and either withdraw or become defensive. It is in this phase that we help students acquire the tools to become independent learners and expand their intellectual capacity. This alliance will allow cognitive insight to happen. Cognitive insight is about making the invisible visible so the teacher is able to get a better understanding of the student's thinking routines. In the process, the student becomes more aware of his own learning moves and is positioned to begin directing his learning. In this phase, both the teacher and student will gain a better sense of the student's particular learning strengths, content misconceptions, and challenge areas. Too often, teachers try to figure out a student's learning process based on test scores or other types of assessments, but these tools don't offer holistic insight into the student's learning moves. Getting dependent learners to be open and vulnerable enough to show you their learning moves begins with rapport.

Rapport and Affirmation

Rapport is generally defined as a "sympathetic connection" with another person that results in that warm, friendly feeling you get when you are in sync. In culturally responsive teaching, rapport is connected to the idea of affirmation. Affirmation simply means that we acknowledge the personhood of our students through words and actions that say to them, "I care about you." Too often, we confuse affirmation with building up a student's self-esteem. As educators, we think it's our job to make students of color, English learners, or poor students feel good about themselves. That's a deficit view of affirmation. In reality, most parents of culturally and linguistically diverse students do a good job of helping their children develop positive self-esteem. It is when they come to school that many students of color begin to feel marginalized, unseen, and silenced.

Affirmation and rapport are really about building trust, not self-esteem. Trust and fear are inversely related; fear activates the amygdala and the release of cortisol. Cortisol stops all learning for about 20 minutes and stays in the body for up to 3 hours. Remember, when the brain feels there's a potential threat based on past experience with a particular person or because of one's own implicit bias or marginalized status in the larger sociopolitical context, the amygdala goes into action and "hijacks" the brain's other systems, throwing the body into defensive fight, flight, or freeze mode. Trust deactivates the amygdala and blocks the release of cortisol.

Trust, therefore, frees up the brain for other activities such as creativity, learning, and higher order thinking. In communal, relational cultures, our own individual sense of survival and well-being is so intertwined with others that we have trained our safety-threat detection system to be on the alert in social settings for any hint of psychological or social threat that might lead us to being shamed, ostracized, or rejected by the group. Keep in mind, the brain experiences social pain—not connecting with others or being rejected by them—in the same way it experiences physical pain. The same areas in the brain light up whether we stub our toe or get rejected.

Most often mistrust builds because a student or parent doesn't feel acknowledged, affirmed, or cared for. I remember having a conversation with a teacher who could not figure out why her relationship with her African American students felt strained. She was especially troubled that several African American girls in her class had refused to participate in a mask-making activity in which the kids placed plaster strips across their face all the way up to their hairline. One girl spoke up and told the teacher that her mother would be upset with her if she got water or the grainy plaster in her hair. The teacher causally dismissed their concerns and insisted they do the activity along with everyone else. The teacher was unfamiliar with the significance of hair in African American culture—how it's cared for, its connection to self-esteem and self-expression.

In turn, she missed an opportunity to affirm the students' cultural needs by simply making scarves available in the classroom when doing activities with water, sand, or any other substance that might mess up their hair. Whether it's being insensitive to Muslim students fasting during Ramadan by having a class party with food and drink or ignoring a low-income family's ability to provide money for a field trip, these small actions chip away at trust and personal regard that are at the core of authentic relationships. This lack of care leads to mistrust, which, over time, can put students (and parents) on the defensive. This underlying mistrust is the reason some parents seem antagonistic. They become defensive and protective based on the perception that the teacher doesn't care.

Core Practices: Affirmation and Validation

In the inner circle of the Ready for Rigor framework, affirmation and validation are two practices that undergird all efforts to operationalize personalization and rapport building. Affirming is simply acknowledging the personhood of each student, appreciating all aspects of them especially those culturally specific traits that have been negated by the dominant culture. Validation, on the other hand, is your explicit acknowledgment to students that you are aware of the inequities that impact their lives. In the next chapter, we will look at the concept of validation in more depth.

Building Trust and Rapport

You can try to speed the trust-building process, but feeling connected grows slowly and requires time for people to get to know each other. It happens in those small day-to-day interactions as a student comes into the classroom, when you pass him in the hallway or on the playground. It happens in the quiet exchanges we have with a student during an activity or with our subtle body language, whether it's a head nod, a quick smile from across a room, or a gentle hand on a student's shoulder when he is struggling with completing his work. Students will begin to feel cared for when they recognize and experience familiar forms of affection and nurturing.

Where to start: Trust begins with listening

The most powerful way to build rapport is by practicing what Reggio Emilia practitioners call a *pedagogy of listening*. Listening communicates a sense of respect for and an interest in the student's contributions.

Research says that 70% of communication is nonverbal. So listening doesn't just mean hearing the words but listening to the emotional quality of the conversation. This seems simple, maybe too simple and obvious.

Janice was a third-grade teacher I met when I was asked to work with an instructional leadership team at Storybrook Elementary School that wanted to get some traction with culturally responsive teaching in their classrooms. Up until this point, it had been hit and miss. Janice knew something was not clicking between her and her students. Because of it, every day, she said, seemed long and uninspired. At first she wasn't convinced about focusing on building rapport with students because she saw it as some touchy-feely performance she had to do every day to get kids to pay attention. I coached the team to understand rapport in a different way based on neuroscience, sociocultural learning theory, and findings from teachers successful with culturally and linguistically diverse students. Janice agreed to restructure parts of her instructional day to make time for relationship building but wasn't sure where to start. Before trying to make a connection with students by being friendlier or sharing more of herself, I suggested she do something else—start with listening.

Because there was a schoolwide effort at Storybrook to use conferencing to talk about student writing, Janice decided to devote the first five minutes of every student writing conference to two simple questions: "How are you?" and "What are you excited about these days outside of school?" She let students talk. She made it clear to students that what they had to say was important. She reported back that at first students were not used to being listened to. They just sat in silence thinking it was some type of test. Finally by the end of a month, she had learned a great deal about her students during their "little chats," as she called them. Janice said the sense of connection and rapport spilled over into other classroom activities. Simply setting time aside to listen with her full attention helped generate rapport. Practicing a pedagogy of listening may be simple but it isn't always easy. Unfortunately, the kind of empathetic, attentive listening that builds rapport is not what we typically do in most classrooms on a day-to-day basis.

Figure 5.1 Listening With Grace

- Give one's full attention to the speaker and to what is being said
- Understand the feeling behind the words and be sensitive to the emotions being expressed
- Suspend judgment and listen with compassion
- Honor the speaker's cultural way of communicating

Using Trust Generators to Build Rapport

In addition to building trust through acts of caring and authentic listening, we can build trust by being more authentic, vulnerable, and in sync with our students. According to researchers, there is a set of actions that help us make more intimate connections with one another and opens the door for building trust (Brafman & Brafman, 2011). I call them *trust generators.*

Figure 5.2 Trust Generators

Trust Generator	Definition	What It Looks Like
Selective Vulnerability	People respect and connect with others who share their own vulnerable moments. It means showing your human side that is not perfect.	Sharing with a student a challenge you had as a young person or as a learner. Sharing new skills you are learning and what is hard about it. The information shared is selective and appropriate.
Familiarity	People develop a sense of familiarity with someone who they see often in a particular setting such as at a bus stop every day or in the café on a regular basis.	Crossing paths with a student during recess or lunch. Bumping into students and their families at a community farmer's market or at a local park. Attending community events that you know the student may have attended.
Similarity of Interests	People create a bond with others who share similar likes, dislikes, hobbies, and so forth. This common affinity allows a point of connection beyond any obvious racial, class, or linguistic differences. This plants the seed of connection in the relationship.	Sharing hobbies, sports, or other things you like that are similar to a particular student's interests. Also sharing social causes that you are passionate about, such as saving the environment or caring for animals.
Concern	People connect when another shows concern for those issues and events important to another, such as births, illnesses, or other life transitions. This plants the seed of personal regard.	Remembering details from a student's life. Demonstrated by asking follow-up questions about recent events.
Competence	People tend to trust others who demonstrate they have the skill and knowledge, as well as the will, to help and support them. This plants the seed of confidence in others.	Students trust the teacher when the teacher demonstrates the ability to teach effectively or make learning less confusing, more exciting, and more successful.

The trust generators are universal in their ability to help us feel an instant sense of connection. How we go about using them is as unique as our fingerprints. It depends on your personality, experience, the age of the children you teach, and your own understanding of their culture, to name a few. That's why you have to give some thought to how you would approach it. There is no formula.

Let's look at how we might use selective vulnerability. Practicing vulnerability requires that we be willing to let down our guard a bit. The most powerful thing we can do to create a culture of caring is to allow ourselves to be seen as human beings, not just in our role as teachers. Psychologists have long known that self-disclosure is one of the hallmarks of intimate, trusting relationships. There is considerable evidence that teachers, leaders, and other authority figures who disclose part of their authentic selves to students or employees build not only trust but generate greater cooperation and teamwork within a group as well (Offermann & Rosh, 2012).

Selective vulnerability is best employed through storytelling. Turns out that storytelling is one of the universal ways people connect and get to know each other around the world. The human brain is hardwired for stories. Long before humans developed writing they passed down their history, culture, and traditions orally through stories. Across cultures, stories have many characteristics in common. Every culture uses stories to entertain, get to know each other, or pass on wisdom. It is not surprising therefore that neuroscience is beginning to find that our brain reacts to a story in a particular way.

For example, when we tell stories to others, the brains of the people listening synchronize with the storyteller's brain. Uri Hasson and his colleagues from Princeton (2010) found that similar brain regions in the prefrontal cortex were activated in both the listener and the storyteller. He calls it "neural coupling," similar to what mirror neurons do. His research suggests that storytelling creates a much deeper connection between people and actually builds empathy and trust. Small talk and general chit-chat fit in this category of trust-building communication. Researcher Jeremy Hsu found personal stories and small talk make up 65% of our conversations. Sharing your story with students makes you more human and vulnerable.

Ways to Put Selective Vulnerability in Action

- Tell your story by weaving it into your lesson—what were you like as a student? What were your favorite subjects? What were some challenges? Bring in pictures of yourself as a child or during your school days.

- Share a new skill or process you are learning—not the finished product but the less-than-perfect beginning and middle parts.
- Share your interests with the whole class and then find fellow fans among individual students with whom you share an interest in the same sports teams, movies, or hobby.
- Bond over a local social cause that means something to you. Let students make a connection to what is important to the community and to you.

Use the worksheet below (Figure 5.3) to reflect on how you might use the trust generators to build a more authentic connection with your students.

Assessing the State of Rapport in the Classroom

Our ultimate goal is to position dependent learners so that they will take the intellectual risk and stretch into their zone of proximal development (ZPD). That's the point of rapport—building trust is designed to help dependent learners avoid the stress and anxiety that comes with feeling lost and unsupported at school.

Figure 5.3 Points of Connection Worksheet

My Points of Connection	
• *What do you see as the best points of connection you can make with your students?* • *In the space on the right, identify a few experiences or stories you might share based on some combination of the trust generators.*	
Trust generators to consider • **Selective Vulnerability** • **Familiarity** • **Similarity & Interests** • **Concern** • **Competence**	

Life in the classroom is often so busy that we aren't always aware of the small interactions that chip away at trust and rapport. It's important to not assume everything is fine. Remember that we are trying to make "the familiar strange" in an effort to gain a deeper awareness of the quality of trust between you and your students. So, what is the current reality? Like Janice, you have to step back and get a better sense of the state of rapport and trust between you and students who are different linguistically and culturally.

How do you find out? Take an inquiry stance. Collect some data on a small group of students rather than trying to assess the class as a whole all at once. Focus in on one or two students we commonly call *focal students*, to get a more intimate view. Use the data to illuminate unconscious patterns in your interactions. Spend about a week or two tracking the quality of the interactions with your dependent learners, especially those that are culturally and linguistically diverse. I asked all members of the Instructional Leadership Team at Storybrook Elementary to track the quality of their interactions with students for two weeks with a simple tally sheet (Figure 5.3). At the end of two weeks, they were quite surprised that the assessment in their heads didn't match the data they collected. One teacher thought she had interacted with her dependent learners quite a bit when in reality she went through most days not even exchanging a word or glance with them. Another teacher realized that she was labeling an interaction as positive because she was using a nice tone of voice. In reality, it was a negative interaction because she was always pointing out to one particular student what he was doing wrong and how he was off-task, never highlighting when he was on task.

Here are some steps for assessing current reality in your classroom.

Identify a specific student you would like to have a better learning partnership with. That student should be representative of a similar group of students in the classroom. What you learn in building a better relationship with this one focal student can be easily applied to other students.

Assess the quality of your relationship with your focal student. Think about how you and your focal student currently interact with each other. Reflect on the following questions and be honest with yourself. Set an intention for what you would like to be true in the future.

Create a system to help you look closely at and listen carefully to your focal student. It seems almost impossible to pay attention to every student in the classroom all the time. That's why you need a system for gathering information about individual students so that you begin to feel you know them personally.

Try "kidwatching." Literacy educator, Yetta Goodman popularized the term in the 1980s as part of a literacy strategy, but the practice has its roots in Montessori and multicultural education. Rather than try to notice every student every day, you select 3–5 students to watch over the course of a week and make notes about each student. Choose a simple system to make note taking easy. Some teachers use index cards, with a card or two for each student. Others use sticky notes. You can plan your observations around social or academic tasks depending on what information you'd like to gather. Over the course of several weeks you should have a great deal of information about your focal students.

Keep track of student responses over time. In the activity of the classroom, it is easy to miss the small signals that trust is growing. Be sure to track your attempts to connect with your focal students and their responses. Think about what adjustments you want to make and track those as well. The goal is to pay attention to this blooming relationship in a new way. Keep a journal. Keep note cards in your desk. Record a voice memo on your smart phone. Whatever way is most convenient for you will work.

You can use a tally sheet like the one in Figure 5.4 to track the number of positive interactions, negative interactions, and neutral interactions. A positive interaction is when the reason you are talking with the student is to show care, affirm him, or simply say hello, while a negative interaction is when you are reprimanding or redirecting the student. Remember that, no matter how upbeat your tone of voice is, if the intention is to point out something the student is not doing, it is a negative interaction.

Crunch the numbers and analyze the data. Once you have tracked your student interactions for a given time period, review it to get a sense of the big picture. How many times did you have a positive interaction? How often did you redirect the student's behavior, give him a verbal warning, or give him "the look"? When analyzing your data, ask yourself if it matches what you imagined was happening. There should be at the very least a 2:1 ratio of positive to neutral or negative interactions. Usually teachers find that they are not having as many positive interactions as they thought. Be sure to analyze the nature of the interactions: When did more positive interactions take place? Why were you having a negative interaction? What was the student's reaction in either case?

Based on your findings, identify one small change you can make to build trust with your focal student. Think about one small change you would like to make that you believe would shift the nature

Figure 5.4 Rapport Interaction Tally Tracking

Mark each time you have an encounter with your focal student. Indicate with a P, 0, or N whether the encounter was positive (P), neutral (0), or negative (N). Make brief notes describing the encounter—what type of interaction.

Dates	Interactions (Tally with P or N)	Notes

of your interactions. Think about the elements of the learning partnership and building rapport. How might you generate more trust? How might you show up differently? Remember that the burden is on you to change the nature of the relationship and build trust between you and your students.

Track the impact of the one small change you made. Once you decide what changes you'd like to make, be sure to track the impact of those changes. If it seems to be leading to positive changes, then continue. If not, do more inquiry and figure out why. The important thing is to practice ongoing inquiry and reflection as you make small adjustments. The goal is to be deliberate and focused.

Operationalizing Rapport Strategies

Once you have assessed what needs to improve in terms of building trust with students, you will want to think about ways to make it happen organically as well as in more structured ways. Here are some suggestions.

Express care in nonverbal ways that shows your concern. Practice listening with grace—communicating nonverbally as a sense of warm concern, openness, attunement to the other, and nonjudgment. Give the student your attention. No multitasking. Look at him directly. Use body language, facial expressions, and hand gestures to convey your attention. Note your posture and make sure it is open and inviting. Get down on their level when possible. Be selectively demonstrative. A pat on the back, a fist bump, or a high five goes a long way in communicating caring and encouragement.

Find time to play and have fun as a class. Practice creating time to just hang out in class—socializing with no other purpose but to connect and nurture relationships. It might be having students perform skits or tell jokes during a "brain break." Laughing produces endorphins, those feel-good chemicals in our brain. It might be sharing a meal together as a class.

Commit to practicing affirmation. Make a commitment to finding something to affirm in each student related to his racial, culture, gender, or linguistic identity. It's common in our individualistic dominant culture to praise students mostly for what they do. On the other hand, in more communal cultures it is more important to recognize and appreciate who the child is and the unique contributions he makes to community life. The important point here is to develop the intention to accentuate the positive in every student, even those that you have yet to develop a connection with or who behave in ways that feel challenging.

Find ways to routinely let each student know that you see who he is, including aspects of his cultural identity. As important as it is for students to be known by their teachers, it is equally important that they know that you know and value them. Recognize those characteristics, attributes, and behaviors that have been portrayed in the larger society as negative or bad, such as hairstyles, energetic and lively style. It can be simply noticing or complementing a new hairstyle. Stay away from stereotypical complements, such as what a good athlete the student is. This is a great place to remind ourselves that the greater sociopolitical context that students exist in tried to limit their possibilities and life options.

Show appreciation for students' native language, especially the proverbs, adages, and poetry that are passed from generation to generation. Use simple phrases or words in their native language as class words to signal transitions from one activity to another or get their attention for announcements. Put the proverbs and inspirational sayings on bulletin boards in the classroom.

IMPLICATIONS FOR SUPPORTING DEPENDENT LEARNERS AND BUILDING INTELLECTIVE CAPACITY

Building rapport with culturally and linguistically diverse students is essential if we want to improve their learning and guide them to do more rigorous work. Remember that we want to partner with students in a new way so that they eventually can take ownership of their learning. But it begins with being more authentic ourselves. Building trust is an important goal in culturally responsive teaching because it paves the way for us to lead students into their zone of proximal development. Still we have to be prepared for students to be skeptical and slow to embrace this new relationship. Practice, persistence, and patience. Trust builds slowly.

CHAPTER SUMMARY

- Because our safety-threat detection system is continuously scanning for potential social-emotional threats, it is the job of the culturally responsive teacher to build trust and rapport in order to reassure our students that they are safe and cared for.

- Culturally responsive teaching that supports dependent learners requires a learning partnership that includes both rapport and alliance.
- Relationships are the cornerstone of culturally responsive teaching.
- It requires a new type of relationship we call a learning partnership.

INVITATION TO INQUIRY

- How would you characterize your relationship with students of color, English learners, or other students who are different from you?
- How can you learn more about what would help your students feel safe and trusting from their perspective and experiences?
- How do you create a sense of trust and safety in your relationship with your students? Do you do this deliberately or randomly?
- See your students in a new light: Where do they excel? What are they expert in?
- Build an asset-based profile of your dependent learners.
- Find out what trust/rapport looks like in your students' respective cultures. Identify commonalities and differences.
- How would you manage potential cultural conflicts around respect and trust?

GOING DEEPER

- *Trust and School Life: The Role of Trust for Learning, Teaching, Leading, and Bridging* (2014) by Dimitri Van Maele, Patrick B. Forsyth, and Mieke Van Houtte
- *Choice Words: How Our Language Affects Children's Learning* (2004) by Peter H. Johnston
- *Fires in the Middle School Bathroom: Advice for Teachers from Middle Schoolers* (2009) by Kathleen Cushman and Laura Rogers
- *Click: The Forces Behind How We Fully Engage with People, Work, and Everything We Do* (2010) by Ori Brafman and Rom Brafman

6 Establishing Alliance in the Learning Partnership

Becoming an Ally to Help Build Students' Independence

Every child deserves a champion: an adult who will never give up on them, who understands the power of connection and insists they become the best they can possibly be.

—Rita Pierson, Educator of 40 years and a staunch antipoverty advocate

In the first part of the learning partnership, the focus is on creating a sense of connectedness with students who come from a relationship-oriented culture. In this chapter, we continue to explore the Learning Partnership quadrant of the Ready for Rigor frame, with a particular focus on the second part of the equation—building an alliance with students. Ladson-Billings (2009) and others emphasize that the point of culturally responsive teaching isn't just about getting along with students but to use that connection to stretch and empower them as learners. According to Gay (2010), this is the ultimate goal of the culturally responsive teacher: to provide resources and personal assistance so students cultivate positive self-efficacy beliefs and a positive academic mindset. As she says, "loving children should not become a proxy for teaching them" (p. 53).

From the beginning, I have tried to make the point that as culturally responsive teachers, we have a particular duty to help dependent learners build their intellective capacity so that they are able to do more independent learning and higher order thinking. As much as we want students to take responsibility for their own learning from the start, they cannot do that without help in the beginning.

James Banks, the father of multicultural education (2002) asserts that if education is to empower culturally and linguistically diverse students, it must be transformative. Being transformative means helping "students develop the knowledge, skills, and values needed to become social critics who can make reflective decisions and implement their decisions into effective personal, social, political, and economic action" (p. 131). Empowerment also can be described as student academic competence, self-efficacy (belief in one's ability), and initiative. This empowerment, according to Edmund Gordon (2004), co-author of *All Students Reaching the Top*, begins with helping marginalized students increase their intellective capacity. But for this to be true, we know students must believe they can succeed at learning tasks and have the motivation to persevere through challenging work. This is the essence of academic mindset. Academic mindset is defined as a student's attitudes, beliefs, and dispositions about school, learning, and his capacity as a learner that are associated with effort, perseverance, and positive academic achievement (Snipes, Fanscali, & Stoker, 2012).

That is why the second part of the learning partnership, *alliance*, focuses on helping the dependent learner begin and stay on the arduous path toward independent learning. An alliance is more than a friendship. It is a relationship of mutual support as partners navigate through challenging situations.

WHY MARGINALIZED DEPENDENT LEARNERS NEED AN ALLY

I met tenth-grader Tyree when I was working with a secondary English Language Arts teacher who had been assigned to what her school district called a "strategic reading class." The strategic reading class was made up of ninth and tenth grade students, largely African Americans with some Latino students, the majority boys who were reading several years behind grade level. Most of them read at the third to fourth grade level. Tyree's teacher, Marci and I were beta testing a literacy curriculum I was developing to accelerate high school students' reading development. Tyree read at the third grade level, but was naturally smart and a bit of a ham. But reading is the primary vehicle for taking in new knowledge in school after fourth grade, and because of his low skills, Tyree had fallen way behind.

His academic challenges weren't just that he couldn't read but that his background knowledge was shallow and his academic vocabulary was small. He couldn't do complex analytical work. Tyree was always up for trying out the learning tools and games I brought for the class to test. I could tell his slow reading frustrated him. He didn't even try when asked to read a complex grade level text. Instead, he feigned disinterest and said this was boring and a waste of time. Tyree was a dependent learner in need of an ally like his teacher, Marci. She didn't blame the students for their reading problems but she didn't sugar coat things either. She pushed them to roll up their sleeves and work to become better readers. In turn, she rolled up her own sleeves right alongside them to find the right tools and most effective strategies. She was their ally.

The alliance phase of the learning partnership speaks to the realities of education in the sociopolitical context that creates unequal academic outcomes for students of color, English learners, and poor students. The education system has historically underserved culturally and linguistically diverse students of color. We have acknowledged the achievement gap that has left many of them with lower skills, unable to do higher order, academically challenging work. Because of institutional inequities, these students have underdeveloped "learn-how-to-learn" skills as well as weak foundational skills in reading and analytical writing (Boykin, Tyler, & Miller, 2005).

As a result, many students go from grade to grade, like Tyree, without becoming proficient readers, writers, or mathematicians. Their awareness of their own lack of academic proficiency leads to a lack of confidence as learners. Unfortunately, many culturally and linguistically diverse students start to believe these skill gaps are evidence of their own innate intellectual deficits. They internalize the negative verbal and nonverbal messages adults at school send to them in the form of low expectations, unchallenging remedial content, and an overemphasis on compliant behavior (Solorzano & Yosso, 2001).

On the inside, many students of color become discouraged and disengaged. In high school, we see them in the back of the classroom, hoodies pulled over their heads, head on the desk napping during the lesson, or painting fingernails. While on the outside, some teachers interpret this behavior as a lack of motivation and a cultural lack of investment in education. What looks like lack of motivation is in reality the student losing hope that anything can ever change because the academic hurdles seem insurmountable (Cammarota & Romero, 2006; Duncan-Andrade, 2007; Quiroz, 1997).

For dependent learners, this can lead to **learned helplessness**. According to Martin Seligman (2006), learned helplessness is the student's belief that he has no control over his ability to improve as a learner. Because he doesn't believe he has the capacity, he doesn't exert any effort when faced with a challenging work assignment or a new skill to develop. Think of learned helplessness as the opposite of having an academic mindset.

Research finds that unconsciously teachers reinforce learned helplessness among low-performing students of color. I remember a bilingual teacher in a meeting putting it succinctly: "When a teacher expresses sympathy over failure, lavishes praise for completing a simple task, or offers unsolicited help, you send unintended messages of low expectations."

The student with this limited outlook believes effort is useless. He begins to cover up, hide, or act out because he believes failure on an assignment or task might expose him as "dumb" to his peers, leaving him vulnerable to teasing and being ostracized. This is likely to trigger an amygdala hijack. Or it might trigger what former Stanford professor and education researcher, Claude Steele calls **stereotype threat**. Stereotype threat is a type of racially charged amygdala hijack. It happens when a student becomes anxious about his inadequacy as a learner because he believes his failure on an assignment or test will confirm the negative stereotype associated with his race, socioeconomic status, gender, or language background (i.e., Black kids aren't good at math; Spanish speakers can't develop academic language). This type of anxiety attack can also be a form of **internalized oppression,** whereby the student internalizes the negative social messages about his racial group, begins to believe them, and loses confidence. In the classroom, anxiety interferes with his academic performance by releasing the stress hormone cortisol, which in turns reduces the amount of working memory available to him to do complex cognitive work. It also inhibits the growth of the student's intellective capacity.

VALIDATING STUDENTS' EXPERIENCES

Learned helplessness is just another form of hopelessness. The alliance phase of the learning partnership provides an opportunity for teachers to restore hope for struggling students left on the wrong side of the achievement gap. It begins with practicing validation. Validation simply means that we acknowledge two things. First, we acknowledge the realities of inequity that impact students in and out of school. It could be acknowledging that students of color have historically been treated differently at school. Or it can mean that their culturally different ways of learning are often mistaken for intellectual deficits. Often in an effort to be color-blind, some teachers downplay or trivialize subtle but persistent microaggressions directed at culturally and linguistically diverse students on a daily basis. For students, these situations cause stress and emotional pain. As an ally, we have to let them know they are not crazy. Inequity is real. Second, it's a chance to validate the personhood of the student and legitimize those ways of speaking or being that have been branded "wrong" in mainstream school culture. Validating students is the first step toward empowering them. Ladson-Billings (2009) says that empowerment through validation is a critical feature of culturally responsive teaching because it helps restore students' sense of hope (Figure 6.1). Restoring hope is one of the main jobs for the teacher as ally in the learning partnership (Duncan-Andrade, 2007).

Being hopeful can be hard if as social justice educators, we continually beat the drum of oppression and social inequity. Culturally and linguistically diverse students know this reality already. Instead, we should focus on highlighting a community's resiliency and vision for social change. Culturally and linguistically diverse students are not helpless victims. They come from communities with a rich history of being the catalyst for social justice movements that have changed the face of the world. And that's not hype. It's history. Ghandi, Martin Luther King, Caesar Chavez, Fannie Lou Hammer, and Dolores Huerta were all merchants of hope within a sociopolitical context that marginalized people of color. Validation has to focus on the resilience of communities of color as exemplified in Maya Angelou's (1994) poem, *And Still I Rise*. In many ways, culturally responsive teachers are merchants of hope in their role as allies in the learning partnership.

WHAT IS AN "ALLIANCE"?

The concept of working alliance grows out of the fields of counseling and coaching. Psychologist Edward Bordin (1994) analyzed the special relationship between counselor and client and identified a unique, collaborative relationship he called a *therapeutic alliance* between the person in need of change and the person there to help support the change process. It has three essential components:

Figure 6.1 Categories of Hope

Not all hope is helpful. Duncan-Andrade highlights the difference between false hope that is superficial, leading to no real change in teaching or learning and critical hope that is realistic about inequities and leverages teacher and student energy.

False Hope	Critical Hope
Hokey Hope	**Material Hope**
This type comes from blind optimism that ignores the laundry list of inequities that impact the lives of culturally and linguistically diverse students inside and outside the classroom when the evidence does not warrant such optimism.	This type comes from the sense of control young people have when they are given the resources to "deal" with the forces that affect their lives. Quality teaching is the most significant "material" resource we can offer culturally and linguistically diverse students.
Hope Deferred	**Socratic Hope**
This type comes from a focus on idealistic socioeconomic changes in society such as ending all poverty—before we can help students. Recognition of social and educational inequities leads to unrealistic hope for change in a distant future.	This type comes as teachers and students examine their lives and actions within an unjust society and allow their pain to pave the path to justice, self-determination, and collective action through academic excellence. The righteous indignation or so-called student "hostility" it generates is seen as a strength to be channeled into positive action and engagement.

Source: Adapted from "Note to Educators: Hope Required When Growing Roses in Concrete," by Jeffery Duncan-Andrade, 2009. *Harvard Review.*

- A shared understanding and agreement to tackle a specific goal
- A shared understanding and agreement about the tasks necessary to reach the goal along with confidence that these activities will lead to progress
- A relational bond based on mutual trust that creates an emotional connection and sense of safety for the client in order to do the hard work necessary to reach the goal

Bordin explains that what makes a therapeutic alliance unique is the reality that working to change or improve in an area will mean working on our weaknesses and that working on these weak areas will definitely trigger the amygdala's fight or flight response in the client's brain, leading to defensive behaviors such as acting out or shutting down. He points out that taking on these tasks will test their bond. But because of the skill and commitment of the ally, the client is able to manage his emotions and shift to a more receptive mindset. This mindset allows the client to stretch himself. In the end, the client expands his capacity. This is why, he says, the client has to have deep trust in his ally and a sense of safety within their relationship. When a client has little trust in the person supporting him through the task and has little or no faith in that person's ability to help him improve, then the client becomes reluctant. While he may go through the motions of working toward change, he isn't able to commit 100% to the process out of fear and lack of trust.

I first recognized the need to establish a similar type of alliance with my students when I was a new high school writing teacher. I was confident in my content knowledge about the different elements of writing and how to teach so students learned to be competent writers. Despite my confidence in my pedagogy, I ran up against something I didn't expect: resistance from my struggling students. It wasn't that they lacked confidence in my ability. It was that they lacked confidence in their own ability. I realized that they were dependent learners who didn't believe they were capable of figuring out how to write well. It was as if I was asking them to go out on a limb and risk their safety. Resistance came in a variety of forms. Some cried. Others got defensive. Others simply withdrew.

I knew that just marking up their papers or having them write yet another draft of the assigned essay would never get them past this mindset. We needed to partner in a different way. I needed to become their ally so that I could ask them to take new risks in their development as writers. In some cases, we literally shook hands to seal our partnership.

FEATURES OF THE LEARNING PARTNERSHIP ALLIANCE

There are three critical parts patterned on Bordin's idea of therapeutic alliance: *the pact, teacher as ally, and the student as driver of his own learning.*

The Pact. The pact is a formal agreement between teacher and student to work on a learning goal and a relational covenant between them. They each pledge to bring their attention and effort to the pursuit of the goal. Often teachers will put in place learning contracts or IEPs, but these are technical tools focused mainly on compliance. The pact has to be relational as well. It is possible to use the formal process of writing up a learning contract with a student as an opportunity to create a focus on the social and emotional aspects of risk-taking.

Teacher as Ally and Warm Demander. As part of her commitment, the teacher acts as an ally to the student in his quest toward independent learning. In this role, the teacher offers both *care* and *push* as needed. The main focus here is cultivating the skills to push students into their zone of proximal development while helping them manage their emotional response so they don't set off their amygdala. The skills and attributes of **warm demander** pedagogy allow teachers to push students to take more academic risks and gain confidence (Ware, 2006).

Student as Driver of His Own Learning. For his part in the alliance, the student commits to being an active participant in the process and taking ownership of his own learning as he works toward his learning goals.

CREATING THE PACT

When I first began the practice of developing a pact with my writing students, I struggled with how to make it feel like an opportunity rather than a punishment. I realized that it meant finding a learning target that would allow the student to experience success but was significant because it set him up for seeing immediate results in other areas of his writing. It also had to be something that the student felt challenged by but wouldn't shut him down. This meant we had to talk about what felt like his strong areas and what he saw as hard or confusing.

It was important to talk *with* the student, not *at* him about taking up this challenge. Make space during your conversations for the student to share his thoughts. Provide open-ended questions and lots of wait time. Students, especially struggling students, are not used to being asked their opinion or to be reflective. You are shifting the power dynamics with the creation of a pact—not power *over* the student but as master instructional coach Jim Knight (2013) says in *Impactful Instruction*, power *with* the student. Here are some tips for getting the Pact off to a good start.

- *Ask the student to identify what he thinks is getting in the way for him around a specific learning target.* It is amazing how accurate students are in identifying where learning breaks down for them or where they feel stuck.
- *Together select a learning target that is small, specific and significant.* Identify a fundamental subskill that has the potential to allow a student to unlock other areas. For example, I realized one of my students didn't understand his long vowels. This impacted his reading fluency, which reduced his comprehension of the texts he was expected to

write about. These problems also showed up in his writing too. So that was our goal: internalize all the long vowel variations.

- *Set a deadline* for mastering the learning target.
- *Set up benchmarks* to check on progress and offer corrective feedback.
- *Share what you are willing to do as the student's ally.* Let him know you are his partner in this process. Be specific about how you will support him.
- *Be explicit about your belief in his capacity to master this learning target.* Make this authentic. Students are good at sniffing out fake flattery. Share the information you've learned about the student's strengths during your rapport-building phase. Help the student understand that you really believe in him.
- *Forewarn him that you will ask him to stretch himself* and that it will feel uncomfortable, but that you are there to support him. Help the student understand this point by drawing a comparison between sports or another skill he has mastered outside of school such as learning to play an instrument.
- *Ask him to explicitly name what he intends to do as part of the partnership to meet this challenge.* Once he's answered, offer two or three other ways he can take responsibility for his own learning.
- *Create some type of simple ritual to mark the occasion.* A handshake, fist bump, or high five. A special pencil with an inspirational slogan on it. It is important to cue the brain so that the experience is infused with emotion so the brain remembers. This stimulates the student's RAS and amygdala and reframes the challenge as a positive activity rather than as a potential threat. Now the student will feel excitement and energy rather than anxiety when thinking about this area of learning.
- *Write down key agreements* and notes from the conversation after you end the meeting with the student.

Find a way to organize the classroom schedule so that you can have periodic conferences or check-ins with students. This use of time is an extension of creating a culturally responsive classroom environment. Talk explicitly about joining forces to make progress on a learning goal within a specific period of time. For example, in three weeks, the student will learn the difference between a complete sentence and a sentence fragment, but the teacher commits to providing specific help in the form of appropriate scaffolding, tools, and feedback. This is the "partnership" element in learning partnerships.

BECOMING A WARM DEMANDER

Your role as ally in the learning partnership calls for you to know when to offer emotional comfort and care and when to not allow the student to slip into learned helplessness. Your job is to find a way to bring the student into the **zone of proximal development** while in a state of **relaxed alertness** so that he experiences the appropriate cognitive challenge that will stimulate his neurons and help his dendrites to grow.

To do this, the culturally responsive teacher takes a warm demander stance. Educator Judith Kleinfeld (1975) at the University of Alaska originally coined the term *warm demander* to describe the style of those teachers most effective with Eskimo and Native Indian children from small rural villages attending urban schools in Alaska. Other educators over the years have identified a similar teaching stance among effective teachers of African American and Latino students (Ladson-Billings, 2009; Ware, 2006). Antrop-González and De Jesús (2006) in their research of two Latino community-based high schools defined this characteristic as *hard caring*, "the combination of high expectations for academic performance that teachers place on students and supportive, instrumental relationships between students and teachers." In *Teach Like a Champion* (2010), Doug Lemov calls it "warm/strict." Even movies have immortalized warm demanders on screen like Jaimie Escalante in *Stand and Deliver* (1988), Marva Collins in *The Marva Collins Story* (1981), and ex-Marine turned teacher, LouAnne Johnson played by actress Michelle Pfeiffer, in *Dangerous Minds* (1995).

Earning the Right to Demand

It is easy to think that just being firm and authoritarian is the key to increasing student achievement for marginalized students. Kleinfeld (1972) and others found the opposite was true. Kleinfeld identified two elements that when put together increased the engagement and effort of students who had disengaged because they were English learners and felt like outsiders in the classroom: *personal warmth* coupled with what she called *active demandingness*. Personal warmth is what Gay (2010) labels *care*. Kleinfeld said this element was important to those students in the study because it was consistent with their collectivist cultural worldview and practices that put a high premium on relationships. Active demandingness isn't defined as just a no-nonsense firmness with regard to behavior but an insistence on excellence and academic effort. This unique combination of personal warmth and active demandingness earns the teacher the right to push for excellence and stretch the student beyond his comfort zone.

She noted that these two characteristics stood in contrast to teachers who exhibited some combination of *professional distance* (no focus on rapport) and *passive leniency* (no focus on effort). The chart in Figure 6.2 lays out the characteristics of each combination of characteristics.

Warmth with passive leniency produced the *sentimentalist*, a teacher who is friendly but holds lower standards and expectations for certain students in a misguided attempt not to hurt their self-esteem. The Sentimentalist offers caring without a focus on helping students take on challenging academics. Professional distance coupled with passive leniency creates the *elitist*, a teacher who sees dependent students of color as less intellectual and favors students whom he deems smart and more like him. He makes no effort to help dependent learners grow their intelligence. Then there is the *technocrat*. This teacher focuses on the technical side of teaching and doesn't try to build relationships or help students develop self-confidence as learners. He is successful with independent learners and some dependent learners.

Students interpret the warm demander's mix of care and push as a sign that the teacher "has his back" (Cushman, 2005; Duncan-Andrade, 2009; Obidah & Teel, 2001). Personal warmth and authentic concern exhibited by the teacher earns her the right to demand engagement and effort. Here is where the power of the teacher as ally in the learning partnership is realized. The culturally responsive teacher willingly develops the skills, tools, and techniques to help students rise to the occasion as she invites them to step out of their comfort zone into the zone of proximal development.

Any teacher can become a warm demander, but it is important to know what your inclination is as a teacher (Figure 6.2). For example, are you more inclined to be a technocrat? Then, you will want to work on cultivating authentic personal warmth and rapport with students and express your active demandingness in positive ways. Remember the big idea from Chapter 4: Self-reflection is the key.

GIVING DEPENDENT LEARNERS THE BASIC TOOLS FOR INDEPENDENT LEARNING

As part of my project beta testing prototypes of morphology literacy games in Marci's classroom, we gave Tyree and his classmates simple data collection sheets to keep track of their level of automaticity with recognizing and matching word roots to their meaning. We started with a few

Figure 6.2 Warm Demander Chart

Active Demandingness

 THE WARM DEMANDER

- Explicit focus on building rapport and trust. Expresses warmth through non-verbal ways like smiling, touch, warm or firm tone of voice, and good natured teasing.
- Shows personal regard for students by inquiring about important people and events in their lives.
- Earns the right to demand engagement and effort.
- Very competent with the technical side of instruction.
- Holds high standards and offers emotional support and instructional scaffolding to dependent learners for reaching the standards.
- Encourages productive struggle.
- Viewed by students as caring because of personal regard and "tough love" stance.

THE TECHNOCRAT

- Has no explicit focus on building rapport. Doesn't focus on developing relationships with students, but does show enthusiasm for the subject matter.
- Holds high standards and expects students to meet them.
- Very competent with the technical side of instruction.
- Able to support independent learners better than dependent learners.
- Viewed by students as likeable even if distant because of teacher competence and enthusiasm for subject.

Personal Warmth ← | → **Professional Distance**

 THE SENTIMENTALIST

- Explicit focus on building rapport and trust. Expresses warmth through verbal and nonverbal communication.
- Shows personal regard for students.
- Makes excuses for students' lack of academic performance.
- Consciously holds lower expectations out of pity because of poverty or oppression. Tries to protect students from failure.
- Either over scaffolds instruction or dumbs down the curriculum.
- Doesn't provide opportunities for students to engage in productive struggle.
- Allows students to engage in behavior that is not in their best interest.
- Liked by students but viewed as a push-over.

 THE ELITIST

- No explicit or implicit focus on building rapport or trust.
- Keeps professional distance from students unlike himself.
- Unconsciously holds low expectations for dependent learners.
- Organizes instruction around independent learners and provides little scaffolding.
- Mistakes cultural differences of culturally and linguistically diverse students as intellectual deficits.
- Makes certain students feel pushed out of the intellectual life of the classroom.
- Allows dependent students to disengage from learning and engage in off-task behavior as long as not disruptive.
- Viewed by students as cold and uncaring.

Passive Leniency

diagnostic assessments to establish their baseline in key reading subskills. Then we did a mini lesson on how the brain learns to read to help them understand what the numbers meant so they could help in analyzing their own diagnostic data. The simple act of collecting data to establish a baseline and having some understanding of what those numbers meant was eye opening for them.

To our surprise, they became very interested in knowing how they were improving. They paid attention to their own growth in new ways. While they still struggled with reading, we could see that they now had some motivation to push themselves when playing the games. In some small way, being an active participant in tracking their own growth encouraged them to take more responsibility for their learning.

The ultimate goal as a warm demander is to help students take over the reigns of their learning. This is the social justice aspect of culturally responsive teaching. The first step toward independent learning is acquiring the tools to be more data driven in one's decision-making about learning tactics and strategies. Dependent learners have been conditioned to be passive when it comes to making decisions about their learning moves. They have relied on the teacher to tell them what to do next. If they are to become more independent we have to provide them with the tools. The concrete things they need from their allies are:

- *Kid-friendly vocabulary for talking about their learning moves.* Help them put into their own words concepts such as data, progress, and assessment that are broader than the traditional standardized testing lingo they hear.
- *Checklists to help hone their decision-making skills during learning and focus their attention during data analysis.* Checklists and rubrics act as cognitive scaffolds. For example, Wheeler and Swords (2006) use a process called contrastive analysis to help African American students who speak and write in African American vernacular (AAV) improve their academic writing skills. They provide students with a list of the top ten AAV patterns that they should be on the lookout for and reduce in their writing. By using the checklist students are able to correct their usage during the revision process.
- *Tools for tracking their own progress toward learning targets.* Provide graph paper or tally sheets so they can plot results from various formative assessments and track their growth over time. Help students develop visuals such as graphs or pie charts so they can see their progress at a glance.
- *Easily accessible space to store their data.* Create a physical place in the classroom to keep data they have collected during formative

assessment tasks. Create portfolios that are more than a random collection of artifacts. Include write-ups, students' reflective notes, and their work samples.

- *Regular time to process their data.* Make time for reflection and data analysis often. Protect this time as sacred. Don't let it get whittled away by less important busy work that often takes up time in the classroom. Consider student assessment reflection time as instructional time.

- *Practice engaging in metacognitive conversations* about their learning moves and cognitive strategy as it relates to improving their learning. The teacher can provide sentence frames. Teachers at The Springfield Renaissance School use an interactive process they call debriefing circles as a way for students to talk to each other about what worked and what didn't work to help them complete the assignment.

- *A clear process for reflecting on and acting on teacher or peer feedback.* One of the fastest ways to improve student performance and build independence is to provide the learner with useable, actionable feedback.

THE POWER OF FEEDBACK TO IMPROVE LEARNING

It is not an accident that students become more engaged in their own learning when they are actively involved in tracking their own progress rather than passively filling in bubbles on standardized tests. To survive, the brain depends on getting regular feedback from the environment so that it can adjust its strategy in its effort to minimize threats and maximize well-being. This is *neuroplasticity* in action. Earlier in Chapter 2, we defined neuroplasticity as the brain's ability to grow itself in order to meet the challenges presented to it from the environment. Feedback helps us literally change our minds. Neuropsychologist, Dr. Rick Hanson (2013), in *Hardwiring Happiness* suggests that activities that promote mindfulness and focused attention (like we do when we are reflecting on feedback or analyzing our assessment data) cause the brain to rewire itself and grow by generating more dendrites and laying down more myelin.

Feedback is an essential element in the culturally responsive teacher's arsenal. Too often, culturally and linguistically diverse students who struggle have developed a set of learning moves that aren't effective and they are not sure what's going wrong or what to do about it. They cannot do higher order thinking or complex work if they cannot learn to adjust their learning moves, acquire new ones, or strategize about how to tackle a task.

According to education researchers Hattie and Timperley (2007), feedback is one of the most powerful tools we have to improve learning. The brain needs feedback or it will keep doing the same thing over and over even if that move doesn't result in improved skill or performance. We see dependent learners do this all the time. James Zull (2002), author of *The Art of the Changing Brain,* points out that when students use feedback and are able to improve their performance or understanding, it triggers the brain's pleasure and reward centers, releasing the powerful brain chemical, *dopamine.* This hit of dopamine motivates the student to apply more effort and stick with the task.

Harvard business professor Teresa Amabile (2012) says our confidence and effort grow as a result of what she calls the *progress principle,* the idea that people develop a greater sense of "I can do it" when they are able to confirm they are making progress toward their goal. Her findings are right in line with Rick Stiggins' work on assessment *for* learning. Stiggins and other advocates of **formative assessment** highlight that an assessment activity can help learning if it provides information that teachers and their students can use as feedback to measure progress and to modify their teaching and learning activities (Wiliam, 2004).

And there are fringe benefits. By engaging in frequent feedback cycles that lead to change, teachers deepen and strengthen their learning partnership with the student. The student recognizes the teacher's willingness to help them get better. This builds trust between them.

Contrary to what we may think, simply giving feedback doesn't initiate change. It has to be accepted as valid and actionable by the learner. He then has to commit to using that information to do something different. For dependent learners this can be scary. Part of our role as an ally is to offer emotional support as well as tools. You have to be able to be in conversation with students who are trying to stretch themselves.

Here is one of those fun facts from neuroscience: The very act of reviewing and applying feedback stimulates the growth of neurons and dendrites in the brain. This action grows more gray matter. More gray matter means more brainpower. For the warm demander, the feedback conversation offers an opportunity to engage the student and help him "up his game." But not just any old feedback will do.

Think about how you learned a new skill or got better at an existing one. You were able to get instructive feedback that helped you make specific adjustments rather than evaluative feedback that just told you whether what you did was good or bad but offered no information to get better. You see corrective feedback in action in sports coaching. The player practices and the coach observes, comparing the player's moves to effective execution of the move. Then, the coach steps in and suggests the player lift his elbow when swinging the bat or asks him to flick his wrist when releasing the basketball. The player takes in this information and makes those specific adjustments. Unclear evaluative feedback is likely to only make matters worse for dependent learners.

Figure 6.3 Types of Feedback

Types of Feedback		
Instructive and Corrective	**Advice not Actionable**	**Evaluative not Instructive**
"In the third sentence, you used the wrong punctuation and have a run-on sentence." "When you added *x* to the equation, you didn't follow the correct procedure." "When you are adding two columns of numbers, you are forgetting to carry the number over."	"You need more examples in your report." "Fix your run-on sentences." "Provide more evidence in your paper." "Watch it when you carry your numbers when adding."	"Good job." "This is a C paper." "Nice presentation." "Your addition is sloppy."

Quality feedback has some distinct characteristics:

- **It is instructive rather than evaluative.** The feedback is focused on correcting some aspect of the student's performance—a step in a procedure, a misconception, or information to be memorized. It isn't advice or a grade but some actionable information that will help the student improve. It is important to know the difference between the three types of feedback because not all feedback is actionable.
- **It is specific and in the right dose**. Your feedback should focus on only one or two points. Don't point out everything that needs adjusting. That's overwhelming for a dependent learner and may actually confirm her belief that she is not capable.
- **It is timely.** Feedback needs to come while students are still mindful of the topic, assignment, or performance in question. It needs to come while they still think of the learning goal as a learning goal—that is, something they are still striving for, not something they already did.
- **It is delivered in a low stress, supportive environment.** The feedback has to be given in a way that doesn't trigger anxiety for

the student. This means building a classroom culture that celebrates the opportunity to get feedback and reframes errors as information.

Making Feedback Culturally Responsive: Giving "Wise" Feedback

For feedback to be effective, students must act on it. We have to engage our students' willingness to act on our feedback. By looking closely at their work to understand what they get and identify where they need help, we are listening to our students. Our feedback can communicate to them that we have heard them, and they will be more likely to trust us enough to follow our advice for that sometimes difficult next step. One of the challenges the ally teacher has to confront in the learning partnership is how to give feedback so that it doesn't shut the student down emotionally or create anxiety.

Research by Cohen and Steele (2002) found that students of color often did not receive timely, actionable feedback from their teachers either because the teacher didn't want to hurt the student's feelings or he didn't want to be perceived as prejudiced because he was pointing out errors to a student of color. Cohen and Steele identified two types of feedback students got. One was effective and the other wasn't. The ineffective feedback they called "cushioned feedback." The teacher downplayed the severity of the errors and provided little if any information the student could use to improve his performance. Delpit (1995) talks about this as a common point of disconnection in cross-cultural communications. She points out that "helpers" from the dominant culture who are trying to give feedback become more indirect and less precise in their communication in a misguided attempt to equalize a racial, linguistic, or socioeconomic power difference. It backfires because the student interprets the vagueness as an attempt to hide the truth.

Cohen and Steele recommend an approach they call **wise feedback**. It's different from the typical sandwich feedback model—start with positive feedback, then give the negative or hard feedback, and end with a positive observation or encouragement. Wise feedback is a way of giving feedback that reassures students that they will not be stereotyped or doubted as less capable. Cohen and Steele (2002) suggest that to be helpful, the teacher has to convey faith in the potential of the student while being honest with the student about the gap between his current performance and the standard he is trying to reach. While delivering negative feedback, the wise educator adds three specific elements to her feedback:

- An explicit holding of high standards. This helps the student understand that his or her mistakes are not necessarily a sign of (perceived) low capability but rather a sign of the high demands of the education program or academic task.
- A personal assurance to the student that he is capable and can improve with effort.
- Specific actionable steps to work on.

Over the years, as I've tutored struggling readers and writers, I created a feedback protocol that has evidence of wise feedback. I call it the *asset-based feedback protocol*. Instead of cushioning or softening the feedback by

Figure 6.4 The Asset-Based Feedback Protocol

1. Begin with a check-in. Have a few minutes for reconnecting. Ask about the student and what is going on in his life—how he is feeling.

2. State explicitly the purpose of your meeting and affirming your belief in the student's capacity as a learner. Give evidence by citing progress and growth in other areas.

3. Validate the student's ability to master the learning target while acknowledging high demands of the task. Have the student analyze the task with you. Identify the easy parts and the harder parts.

4. Deliver feedback that is specific, actionable, and timely. Restate what the final goal is and what mastery looks like and then show the student where he is in relationship to the goal.

5. Create space for the student to react to what he has heard and how he feels about it.

6. Give the student specific actions to take to improve: new strategies, instructions on what to tweak during the execution of the task. Give feedback and action steps in writing if possible. Provide some way to track progress.

7. Ask the student to paraphrase what he heard you say—what is wrong, what needs to be fixed, and how to go about fixing it.

8. Offer emotional encouragement and restate your belief in him. It is important not to skip this part, even if the student seems uncomfortable. He is taking it in even if he is playing it cool.

9. Set up a time to follow up and check progress.

making it less precise and vague, feedback is delivered in a more explicit yet affirming way.

IMPLICATIONS FOR SUPPORTING DEPENDENT LEARNERS AND BUILDING INTELLECTIVE CAPACITY

Struggling students need not just an advocate but also an ally. It's important to remember that, because of learned helplessness, low confidence, or a negative academic mindset, on their own dependent learners may not be capable of developing the skills and habits of mind that allow them to take on more rigor. It is critical that they do. Rigorous academic challenges are the key to building more neurons and dendrites.

Having a two-way alliance in the learning partnership is essential. The challenge of moving dependent learners forward doesn't all rest on you. The goal of the learning partnership is to help students become more actively engaged in their own learning. It starts with creating a pact between students and teachers. If you create the right conditions of care and challenge as a warm demander, students will rise to the occasion.

Your task is to think about the tools, tactics, and techniques you need to gather or develop in order to be culturally responsive within the learning partnership.

CHAPTER SUMMARY

- Being an effective culturally responsive teacher means building an alliance with students.
- The teacher in the role of ally is mindful of balancing rigor and expectation with support in order to avoid triggering an amygdala hijack.
- Offering actionable corrective feedback is critical.
- Feedback must be offered in ways that affirm the student's capacity to learn yet is honest in pinpointing where he is in relationship to his goal and offers concrete steps for improving.

INVITATION TO INQUIRY

- Of the four types of teacher, what type are you? What shifts would you have to make in order to become more of a warm demander?
- In what ways are you being an ally to your students?
- What role does feedback play in your instructional practice?

- What type of feedback are you usually giving? Is it evaluative or instructive?
- What might you do differently in offering more wise feedback?

GOING DEEPER

- *Note to Educators: Hope Required When Growing Roses in Concrete* (2009) by Jeffery Duncan-Andrade
- "The Power of Feedback" (2007) by John Hattie and Helen Timperley
- *Opening Minds: Using Language to Change Lives* (2012) by Peter H. Johnston
- *Choice Words: How Our Language Affects Children's Learning* (2004) by Peter H. Johnston
- *Because of the Kids: Facing Racial and Cultural Differences in Schools* (2001) by Jennifer Obidah and Karen Manheim Teel
- The Deeper Learning Series: Debrief Circles: A Peer-to-Peer Feedback Strategy (Video) The Teaching Channel. www.teachingchannel.org

7 Shifting Academic Mindset in the Learning Partnership

Restoring Students' Natural Confidence as Learners

If you can show me how I can cling to that which is real to me, while teaching me a way into the larger society, then and only then will I drop my defenses and hostility, and I will sing your praises and help you to make the desert bear fruit.

—Ralph Ellison

In the last chapter, we looked at the important role you play as an ally in a learning partnership and how to go about building your capacity to stand shoulder-to-shoulder with your students as they work to take over the reigns of their learning. The first step in helping them take greater ownership rests in giving them feedback and space for reflection. But you know what the old adage says: "You can lead a horse to water, but you can't make it drink." In a similar way, we can give our students all the right kinds of feedback and create processes to help them reflect on it, but if we cannot get them to take it to heart nothing will change. To get dependent learners to act on feedback or to be strategic, they have to first believe in themselves as learners.

As warm demanders, our job is to get students to recognize that putting forth the effort is worth the work. We do this by helping each student cultivate an academic mindset. The University of Chicago Consortium on School Research (CCSR) in its report, "Teaching Adolescents to Become Learners: The Role of Noncognitive Factors in Shaping School Performance," defines academic mindset as the "beliefs, attitudes, or ways of perceiving oneself in relation to learning and intellectual work" (p. 28) that motivate students to engage in a learning task (Farrington et al., 2012). Stanford psychologist Carol Dweck (2007) in *Mindset: The New Psychology of Success* points out that what we believe about ourselves as learners and our ability to be effective are the catalysts for learning. Her research supports decades of other research findings that tell us students with positive academic mindsets are more willing to engage, work harder, and persevere during challenging assignments that stretch them.

Figure 7.1 Academic Mindset Components

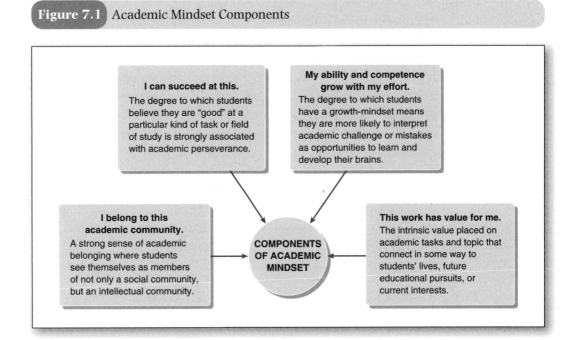

On the other hand, students with negative mindsets are more likely to either act up or zone out in response to their internal belief that they can't be successful. They may put forth effort only to give up quickly when learning gets hard and they realize they don't have the tools to complete the task.

That is what happened to me right after junior high school. I was accepted to attend San Francisco's prestigious public high school, Lowell High. It was the only college prep high school in the school district at the time. The student body was primarily White and Asian, with very few African American, Latino, or Pacific Islander students. From the first day, I felt I always had to prove I belonged there. I questioned if I really did belong there. All my friends had gone to the local high school with the general education or vocational tracks and I felt alone, which didn't help. I remember sitting in my trigonometry class understanding what seemed like every third word the teacher said. The formulas he wrote on the board seemed like chicken scratch. Then I failed the class final exam. That confirmed it for me. I didn't belong at Lowell. I told myself this college prep stuff was for the birds (I am sure my teenaged self used more colorful language) and asked my mother to transfer me. Not knowing how to intervene, she reluctantly sent me to the local high school with all my friends. Despite being a good reader and independent learner, I still experienced self-doubt.

Often we misinterpret a student's self-doubt or negative mindset as a lack of engagement or motivation when we see him exhibiting those common symptoms—zoning out, acting up, or shutting down in class. We then focus on trying to increase engagement with high energy starters such as *call and response* that aren't connected to deeper learning, hoping that it flips some internal switch for the student, leading to a more positive academic mindset, which will in turn transform their academic performance. In reality, we have it backward. What we believe about belonging, effort, and value of the task leads to engagement and motivation.

As culturally responsive teachers, we have to address the real root of the problem—students' self-doubt that leads to a negative academic mindset. This means that as culturally responsive teachers our focus has to be on shifting mindset rather than on trying to force engagement or cajole students' motivation. Students have to become self-motivated. That's one of the hallmarks of an independent learner.

THE NEUROSCIENCE OF ACADEMIC MINDSET

As we try to connect the dots between dependent learners and intellective capacity building, academic mindset is an important dot worth understanding. Teachers hear a lot about it as the source of self-motivation these days but not a lot about what's going on in a student's brain that creates a positive mindset toward learning. Because we don't understand how to develop a positive mindset or shift a negative one, many of our efforts are just trial and error with little lasting impact.

Academic mindset is the result of four conceptual and identity frames all braided together by our older limbic brain to create this thing we call

Figure 7.2 Academic Mindset Cycle Graphic

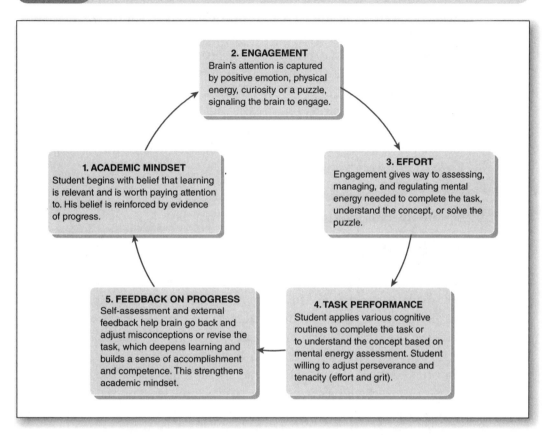

mindset. These four elements make up our internal mindset scripts (schema) that we talked about in Chapter 2:

- Our sense of mastery and competence as learners based on past experience and sense of preparedness
- Our belief in our ability to move about the world freely and control our external world
- Our deep belief in ourself and our ability to achieve what we put our mind and energy toward
- Our explanatory story that we tell ourselves about why we are or aren't competent learners

These elements make up the script that becomes the software that the limbic brain programs into our safety-threat system. It scans the information stored in our hippocampus (our own personal Wikipedia pages) and recognizes patterns over a period of time related to our sense of competence, self-efficacy, and ability to grow as a learner. At a certain point, the brain believes that the same patterns will continue to repeat themselves, so it creates a software program (schema) that will run on autopilot to help us respond to various learning situations consistently, knowing when to pay attention or not, when to put forth any effort or not. The hippocampus feeds this information to the thalamus, our brain's "air traffic controller" and the amygdala, the guard dog. The brain has this script coded into its safety-threat system with instructions to either avoid certain learning situations or to embrace them. The way the brain chooses to interpret and encode this information results in either a **fixed mindset** (won't take a risk) or a **growth mindset** (willing to take a chance).

Sociopolitical Impact on Academic Mindset

Too often, we think of a student's academic mindset as a personal choice or an extension of his family's failure to value education. In reality, schools do a lot more to influence a negative academic mindset than we'd like to admit sometimes. Most schools still have structural inequities that are predictive of who will be a high achiever and who will be a low achiever along racial lines. Unfortunately, over time these structural inequities begin to shape a student's internal story about himself as a learner. The student who is a struggling reader in seventh grade might believe he is just a slow learner. He isn't aware of the policies and practices that led to poor reading instruction in second grade with no interventions to close his learning gaps before he moved to third grade. In addition to policies and practices that limit opportunities, culturally and linguistically diverse students encounter subtle and not so subtle negative messages about their capabilities, the importance of their contributions, and their expected life outcomes (Boykin & Noguera, 2011) from adults in schools and from more privileged students.

Microaggressions and Negativity Bias

The internal scripts students develop that turn into a negative academic mindset or low engagement in the classroom are a result of the everyday microaggressions they encounter. Microaggressions are those small, seemingly innocuous, brief verbal, behavioral, or environmental indignities that send hostile, derogatory, denigrating, and hurtful messages to people of color. They are not overt, racist actions, but small, nonverbal snubs, dismissive looks, gestures, and a condescending tone of voice (Kohli & Solorzano, 2012; Sue et al., 2007) that our neuroception has learned to pick up.

When teachers frame student differences as deficits rather than as assets, a microaggression is ignited for the student. Too often, teachers who are not working to become culturally responsive misinterpret cultural differences as deficits, dysfunctions, or disadvantages in students, leading the teacher to react negatively toward the student rather than respond positively (Ford, Moore, & Whiting, 2006).

Unfortunately, the brain has what is called a *negativity bias*, meaning it remembers and responds to negative experiences up to three times more than positive experiences. Negativity bias was originally designed by the brain to help the RAS be on the lookout for threats to our safety and psychological well-being. It was important back then to remember what happened when we ate the wrong berry or said the wrong thing in public. The brain is still wired to pay more attention to negative experiences. The brain reads these negative microaggressions as feedback from our environment and codes them into our software program, internalizing these messages as mindset. When negativity bias is activated in classrooms, it only reinforces and amplifies a student's negative academic script, leading him to believe school is an unwelcoming place where he cannot be himself.

Here are other forms of microaggressions that show up in schools:

- *Microassaults* involve misusing power and privilege in subtle ways to marginalize students and create different outcomes based on race or class. In the classroom, a microassault might look like giving a more severe punishment to a student of color than his White classmate who was engaged in the same behavior. Or it might look like overemphasizing military-like behavior management strategies for students of color. With younger children, it looks like excluding them from fun activities as punishment for minor infractions.
- *Microinsults* involve being insensitive to culturally and linguistically diverse students and trivializing their racial and cultural identity such as not learning to pronounce a student's name or giving the student an anglicized name to make it easier on the teacher. Continually confusing two students of the same race and casually brushing it off as "they all look alike."
- *Microinvalidations* involve actions that negate or nullify a person of color's experiences or realities such as ignoring each student's rich funds of knowledge. They are also expressed when we don't want to acknowledge the realities of structural racialization or implicit bias. It takes the form of trivializing and dismissing students' experiences, telling them they are being too sensitive or accusing them of "playing the race card."

Setting the Stage for a Mind Shift

Now that we have a better idea of what is going on in the brain, we want to begin to think about how we help students shift their mindset. Before we can help dependent learners expand their intellective capacity by willingly taking on challenging work and growing toward independence, we have to assist them in reprogramming their brain's academic mindset software and rewiring their safety-threat system so that they don't trigger the release of stress hormones every time they try to stretch themselves academically with new challenges.

Validation

In Chapter 5, we looked at affirmation and rapport as keys to establishing a positive cross-cultural relationship with your students. Here we couple validation with academic mindset. As an ally, the culturally responsive teacher validates students' experience in the larger sociopolitical context. We don't trivialize issues of racism, language discrimination, or socioeconomic injustice that show up in the media. Instead, we use these events to remind students that they are not crazy or being overly sensitive when they experience microaggressions.

Self-Efficacy and the Feedback Loop

The key to helping students push back and build a strong academic mindset, especially around effort, is by strengthening what psychologists call **self-efficacy**. Albert Bandura (1986) introduced the idea that self-efficacy, the notion of an "I think I can" philosophy affects how we feel, think, and act as learners. Students' efficacy beliefs are positively associated with how long they will persevere at a learning task. Despite all the focus on grit and perseverance, self-efficacy is at the core of academic mindset, especially elements 2 and 3:

- *My ability and competence grow with my effort.* Students who believe they can increase their academic ability by their own effort are more likely to work toward building competence, more likely to be self-motivating and persistent.
- *I can succeed at this.* Students who believe that they are likely to succeed at a given task are more inclined to put forth effort. Students tend to engage in activities that they feel confident in their ability to complete and tend to avoid those in which they lack confidence.

Rebuilding that "I think I can" attitude begins with helping the student achieve small, incremental success on important tasks. It is important to point out that building self-efficacy isn't just about positive thinking or having the student repeat inspirational affirmations. The brain is a pattern seeker and problem solver. It is happiest when it is making progress toward solving the problem, figuring out the pattern, or completing the task. This builds self-efficacy more than superficial positive thinking activities.

Reframing Mistakes as Information

When dependent learners have a fixed mindset, mistakes are viewed as confirmation of one's lack of ability. As part of building a culture of self-assessment and feedback, we have to help students see errors and mistakes as information to help them improve the outcome next time around. Think about how you will build a classroom culture that approaches mistakes differently. How will students talk about their mistakes? What opportunities will they have to rethink their approach to a task based on what they've learned from past failures? If the student views mistakes as information that help him to be more effective, he develops a growth mindset that is open to applying effort.

The challenge is that in most classrooms mistakes and errors are seen as something bad. While an answer may be wrong, it still can be instructive to the student. This is particularly critical in math and science where a student's low self-efficacy can become a self-fulfilling prophecy. This means the teacher has to talk about errors and mistakes in new ways.

Strategies to Help Shift Mindset

Because only the learner can learn, our role can only be as a coach when trying to get dependent learners to shift their mindset.

Help students create a counter narrative about their identity as learners. As part of a fixed mindset, the dependent student usually has a narrative in his head about who he is as a learner. It's a story he tells himself about why he can't learn, what Seligman calls *explanatory style*. These narratives act like software that program the brain to behave and react in a particular way. Everyone carries a set of narratives that are an extension of our general schema. To help shift their mindset, dependent learners have to develop their own individual counternarratives. This particular narrative is designed to deliberately tell another story, one that runs counter to the

Figure 7.3 Two Mindsets

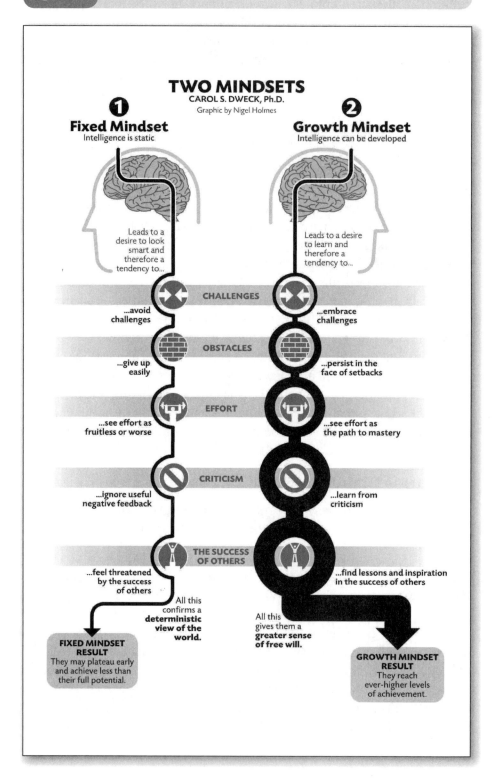

dominant messages a student gets on a day-to-day basis. This new narrative responds to experiences based on reality, not just inspirational positive thinking. Remember that the brain's natural way of making sense of things is through a story structure.

Here is a process to help students craft a powerful collective counter-narrative.

Step 1: Introduce the notion of counter-narratives to the class through stories or poetry. Read an age-appropriate story or poem that offers a different view of the student's cultural characteristics. For example, try classic poetry such as Nikki Giovanni's poem, *Ego Trippin'* (1993) or Sandra Cisneros' *Only Daughter* (1995).

Step 2: Lead a discussion of how the poem's images contrast with the way the students' culture is depicted in the mainstream media.

Step 3: Set up the narrative redesign task as a collaborative writing exercise. Help students identify two or three dominant beliefs that are relevant to academic mindset (i.e., girls aren't good at math).

  —Discuss as a group during morning circle or class advisory time.

  —Create brainstorming time so students can generate one or two points that counter each dominant belief listed earlier.

  —Invite students to weave their new counterpoints into a story format. For example, they now write a new story about how girls *are* good at math using examples from their own life, community, or history.

Use images, quotes, and poetry to ignite student's imagination about what's possible. The limbic region is that part of our brain that connects emotion and cognition. It processes information without words. Instead, it focuses on images and emotions. It processes pictures at twice the speed of words. This is helpful in bypassing the negative self-talk that is part of a negative mindset. Literacy expert Alfred Tatum uses what he calls "poetic broadsides" to get students fired up and connected to their academic mindset. Linda Christensen, author of *Reading, Writing, and Rising Up* (2000), uses poetry as a way to open students to new possibilities.

Find culturally congruent images that communicate a positive sense of triumph, success, and accomplishment. Laminate the images and post them around the room. Have students select one and find a personal connection to the image and then share. Start the lesson with the *Tea Party Protocol* to take advantage of the brain's *primacy-recency effect,* where we tend to remember what comes at the beginning of a learning episode or at the end of it (Sousa, 2001). When the primacy-recency effect is coupled with a strong emotional resonance, the brain begins to integrate those messages as part of its explanatory story. Eventually they become a mantra or empowering manifesto.

Notice and acknowledge students when they are acting according to the elements of academic mindset. Remember that the brain has a negativity bias. As a result, the student will gloss over evidence that he is making progress despite not reaching his goal. As the student's ally, you have to be that voice that cues his brain's reticular activating system to pay attention to these new behaviors. Practice catching students in the act of being self-directed learners or taking intellectual risks. Point out in a matter-of-fact way when you see students who may normally exhibit learned helplessness acting like scholars when they ask thoughtful questions, put forth effort, and learn from their errors.

Help students connect with their current expertise and competencies. Remember what neuroscientists say about "neurons that fire together, wire together." By having students state in writing and share with others their area of expertise, you are helping stimulate those regions of the brain related to self-concept and competency. Have them remember what it felt like to "get good" at their skill or body of knowledge. Ask them to bring this same effort to learning in the classroom. You are helping them make the link between effort and results.

Try the following *Success Analysis Protocol* patterned after protocols used in teacher professional learning communities to help students name their strengths and successes (Figure 7.4).

Help students interrupt negative self-talk. In its efforts to keep us safe, the amygdala tries to dissuade us from taking social or emotional risks. For a dependent learner, trying something new feels risky. These internal messages are designed to keep us safe from venturing too close to the edge of our comfort zone. This safety measure comes in the odd form of negative self-talk. Seligman (2006) says that negative self-talk is part of learned helplessness. Just praising the student or giving him a pep talk won't stop his negative self-talk. You have to show the student how to interrupt these internal statements and replace them with more positive ones.

Use the *Back Talk* strategy. Have the student write down some of the negative statements he makes in class and "talk back" or refute them based on evidence (Figure 7.5).

Figure 7.4 Success Analysis Protocol

1. Have student reflect on and write a short description of the "best learning move" or completed project they are most proud of within the last grading period. Note what it is about the learning experience that made it so successful. Be sure to have them answer the following question as well: "What made this work different from other experiences?" (10 minutes)

2. Have students get into mixed groups of 3. The first person shares their "learning move" or completed project and why it was so successful. (10 minutes)

3. The rest of the group asks clarifying questions about the details of the work. (5 minutes)

4. The group does an analysis of what they heard about the presenter's success and offers additional insights about how this practice is different than other practices. Probing questions are appropriate and the presenter's participation in the conversation is encouraged. (10–15 minutes)

5. The presenter responds to the group's analysis of what made this experience so successful. (3 minutes)

6. Take a moment to celebrate the success of the presenter.

7. Each of the other members of the group takes turns sharing their work in the same manner.

Figure 7.5 Back Talk Strategy

Back Talk Strategy		
Negative Statement (Usually "always" statements)	**Evidence It's Not True** (At least not true all the time)	**Positive Restatement** (Challenge the "always" statement)
"I am not good at math. I never get any math problems right."	"On my last quiz I got 5 problems right out of 9. Before that I got 3 out of 9 correct."	"I am getting better at math. I do get some math problems right."

IMPLICATIONS FOR SUPPORTING DEPENDENT LEARNERS AND BUILDING INTELLECTIVE CAPACITY

One of the realities that we have to embrace as culturally responsive teachers is that the structural inequities in our school systems negatively influence the academic mindset of many of our culturally and linguistically diverse students. Many dependent learners have internalized the messages of not being smart enough. They have begun to believe they are not capable of taking on rigorous academic content. Our task as culturally responsive teachers is to help them shift their mindset by helping them create a powerful counternarrative about who they are as learners.

Shifting a dependent learner's mindset takes more than platitudes and cheerleading. Through the process of validation and critical examination of dominant cultural messages, you can help them develop critical hope and recognize their true potential.

CHAPTER SUMMARY

- Helping dependent learners cultivate an academic mindset is critical in order for them to act on feedback and move toward independent learning.
- Microaggressions trigger an amygdala hijack and negatively impact academic mindset.
- Rebuilding mindset begins with helping students notice their own progress.
- Reframing mistakes as information is an essential part of having a positive academic mindset.

INVITATION TO INQUIRY

- Review your class roster. Put an *F* (for fixed mindset) or *G* (for growth mindset) by students' names. Possible ways to organize the data include the following: *How many of your proficient/advanced students have a fixed mindset? How many of your lower performing students have a growth mindset?*
- Based on what you know about the features of growth mindset, where are your students in relationship to some of those elements?
- How might you be reinforcing a particular mindset without knowing it?
- What are common features of your dependent students' explanatory stories?

GOING DEEPER

- *How Children Succeed: Grit, Curiosity, and the Hidden Power of Character* (2013) by Paul Tough
- *The Will to Learn: A Guide for Motivating Young People* (1998) by Martin V. Covington
- *Drive: The Surprising Truth About What Motivates Us* (2011) by Daniel H. Pink
- *Whistling Vivaldi: How Stereotypes Affect Us and What We Can Do* (2011) by Claude M. Steele

PART III

Building
Intellective Capacity

8 Information Processing to Build Intellective Capacity

Growing Brain Power Through Elaboration

Our brains are magnificent organs for the discovery and creation of meaning. Awake or asleep our brains constantly seek to make sense of inner and outer experience.

—Arthur W. Combs, Educator and Psychologist

I don't divide the world into the weak and the strong, or the successes and the failures, those who make it or those who don't. I divide the world into learners and non-learners.

—Benjamin R. Barber, Political Theorist

Our ultimate goal as culturally responsive teachers is to help dependent learners learn how to learn. We want them to have the ability to size up any task, map out a strategy for completing it, and then execute the plan. That's what independent learners do. Up until this point, we have talked about the necessary conditions that need to be in place in order to focus on building dependent students' cognitive horsepower so that they can easily reach the higher levels of Bloom's taxonomy. On behalf of culturally and linguistically diverse dependent learners, that means paying attention to ways to minimize the impact of school environments that are less than welcoming. All that work to build learning partnerships, become an ally and a warm demander is so that culturally and linguistically diverse students have the space to grow their intelligence. In this chapter, we move from Practice Area II: Learning Partnerships to Practice Area III: Information Processing in the Ready for Rigor framework. We want to look closely at the dimensions of culturally responsive teaching that focus on building intellective capacity through information processing—the student's ability to take inert facts and concepts and turn them into useable knowledge.

Often educators mistake the idea of "using the cultural knowledge, prior experiences and performance style of diverse students" as the need to dress up or disguise a lesson with cultural references to food, holidays, or prominent cultural figures while delivering the lesson in traditional ways—lecture, reading, and testing. We have all seen the math lesson that tries to superficially link math concepts to Egyptians in Africa or Aztecs in Mexico. It doesn't take much to find some straight-laced teacher on You-Tube trying to rap about some historical event as a way to make her social studies lesson "culturally responsive" while her students sit and giggle as passive spectators rather than participate as active learners. As important as including multicultural content is to making learning relevant, it alone doesn't increase brainpower.

Processing information for understanding is very different from simply remembering dates, people, and events. Yet, when I was an instructor at a community college in Washington State, I saw many students who believed that's what learning was. I taught freshman composition and my students were always shocked at the amount of close reading of complex texts they were expected to do. (That's before we called it "close reading of complex texts.") I'd always hear moaning and groaning when we reviewed the syllabus. There was always some bold soul who'd challenge me on this. "I don't get it. What does all this reading have to do with writing?" "If we didn't read, then what would we write about?" I'd ask. They would go along with the program until we began our reading. It was clear some students didn't understand how to process the text or how to extract the author's points and arguments. They didn't have tools or strategies. Most had been allowed to write about their opinions as if they were facts and pass it off as argumentation. When it came to responding to those ideas in writing, there were always tears. At first I couldn't understand why there was so much crying and so many meltdowns. It was just a composition class, but I soon realized many of my community college students, mostly poor working class students and students of color, had not been asked to do this type of work in high school. They didn't have the cognitive tools to complete the task, and they learned I wasn't going to spoon feed it to them. Instead, I set out to help them increase their brainpower by helping them learn to process texts using cognitive strategies and information processing techniques that stretched them into their zone of proximal development.

THE POWER OF ACTIVE PROCESSING

The power of culturally responsive teaching to build underserved students' intellective capacity rests in its focus on information processing. Processing is the act of taking in information with the intent to understand it, relate it to what you already know, and store it in a way so that you can easily retrieve it. For example, imagine you've just been introduced to a new concept in science such as displacement (when the volume or weight of a fluid such as water is displaced by an object of equal weight). Just because you have heard the teacher's lecture or lesson on displacement doesn't mean you've processed it. To process it, you stop, pay attention to the idea, and begin a set of mental operations to understand the concept. You try to relate it to something you've experienced so you think about when you got in the bathtub and the water overflowed. Your brain continues to process the concept until you have an "aha" moment, the proverbial light bulb goes on, and you get it. You understand the concept of displacement both as a concrete event and an abstract idea. This new understanding is now permanently connected to your old knowledge and stored in your memory ready to be used when you need it.

Our ability to process, store, and use information dictates whether we are able to do more complex and complicated thinking in the future because they are the very things that stimulate brain growth. It is precisely explicit information processing that is too often left off the equity agenda for low performing students of color, preventing them from becoming truly independent learners. According to Robert Marzano (2004) in *Building Background Knowledge for Academic Achievement*, the ability to process information effectively can offset other disadvantages such as lack of access to enrichment activities, trips to museums, and other academically oriented experiences that build background knowledge.

Daniel Rigney (2010), author of *The Matthew Effect: How Advantage Begets Further Advantage* points out the negative effects of not having the opportunity to develop key cognitive skills. The cognitively rich will only get academically richer while the cognitively poor will get academically poorer, as small differences in learning abilities such as information process are allowed to grow into large gaps. *The Matthew Effect*, named after the Bible verse found in the Gospel of Matthew, underscores why we won't be able to close the achievement gap and other opportunity gaps if a disproportionate number of children of color are dependent learners. Without greater intellective capacity, dependent learners will never improve their achievement on standardized tests or meet the Common Core standards because they cannot perform the necessary processing on their own.

THE NEUROSCIENCE OF INFORMATION PROCESSING

Culturally responsive teaching offers a way to reintegrate information processing into everyday instruction because many of the learning strategies parents of culturally and linguistically diverse students use at home resemble the cognitive routines taught in advance classes. We will look at those routines later in the chapter. First we need to understand how the brain actually processes information. Think of the brain like a power plant that takes raw material and moves it through a series of filters, blenders, and applications in order to turn that raw material into something useable. Cognitive scientists recognize three stages in the process: *input*, *elaboration*, and *application*. Here is a brief description of what goes on in each stage.

Stage 1: Input. During the first stage, the brain decides what information it should pay attention to. The brain is bombarded with over a billion bits of information per second from the environment. In the classroom, this includes sounds of chairs moving, fellow students whispering behind you, the teacher giving directions, announcements over the PA system, and a host of other things happening. In the middle of a lesson, while taking notes, the student has to decide what to write down, what information to pay attention to. Thanks to the reticular activating system (RAS), the brain is able to filter out a lot of this extraneous input and zero in on what it recognizes as important—something relevant, something that stimulates curiosity, or something that elicits a strong emotional response. Pictures, puzzles, sound, and other attention getters signal to the brain that a particular piece of information is important. If the brain decides to process this information, it routes it through the hippocampus in the limbic brain into the memory system. The first stop is short-term memory where the new information sits while the brain decides if it wants to continue processing it. Think of the short-term memory as a clipboard where you place temporary information. It can only hold a few bits of information, up to seven numbers such as in a phone number. The information can stay there 5–20 seconds before it begins to fade to make room for new information coming in. The hippocampus sends the information along to the elaboration stage if it wants to process it.

Stage 2: Elaboration. If the brain decides it wants to let in this information and seek to understand what it means, it sends the info on to the next phase, elaboration. Elaboration makes material memorable and meaningful. The elaboration stage is where learning for understanding takes place. Cabrera and Colosi (2012) say that elaboration marks the difference between students becoming knowledgeable or "information-filled." The brain moves the information from the clipboard of the short-term memory on to the working memory.

Think of the working memory as a workbench or tabletop. The brain has 5–20 minutes to begin processing the input once it is placed on the tabletop. It is during this stage that the brain is working hard to organize the material into recognizable patterns and to remember it for the future. It is during this stage we introduce culturally responsive processing tools: movement, repetition, story, metaphor, or music to help the brain process. It then begins going through a set of cognitive routines that activate the "firing" of neurons and triggers a cascade of chemical and electrical impulses. If music or some other element is used to help process the information, the neurons connected to that element begin to fire in sync with neurons coded with the new information. As they fire together, they "wire" together, making a permanent association in the brain. This is the main activity of culturally responsive teaching. This mental kneading, massaging, and braiding together of material in an effort to make sense of it and connect it to what the brain already knows stimulates dendrites, those treelike extensions on a neuron that help increase the surface area of the cell body, to grow.

As the brain works to couple the old and new material, it has to periodically stop and cycle down, going into a brief consolidation mode where it stops processing information for a few minutes to let things settle. Our brains can do active processing for 12–20 minutes based on age. For example, in a 40-minute middle school lesson, the brain processes for 12–15 minutes before it cycles down for about 10 minutes. Regardless if the teacher is still talking or not, it will stop paying attention. Then it returns to processing for another 12–15 minutes (Sousa, 2001). It cycles between elaboration and down time to consolidate the information it just processed.

Stage 3: Application. After elaboration, the brain moves to application. The application stage focuses on giving the brain opportunities to apply this new knowledge through deliberate practice and real life application.

Opportunities to apply what we have learned come through place-based learning, project-based learning, or problem-based learning and help solidify learning. The old adage "use it or lose it" applies to this stage of information processing. The brain is working hard to turn those neurons' new dendrites into a permanent neural pathway. We have 24–48 hours to revisit, review, and apply what we have learned in order to make it permanent and move it to long-term memory where it becomes part of our skill set, background knowledge, or conceptual understanding. Every time we think about or use our new knowledge through deliberate practice the new sparse neural pathway that is no more than a footpath soon becomes a well-worn path that allows us to quickly go into long-term memory and retrieve it. As new neural pathways are created, working memory's capacity expands. In addition to strengthening the neural pathways, active, focused practice stimulates the process of myelination. Myelin, that fatty coating on the outside of the neuron, acts as an electrical conduit that allows neurons to "fire" faster and stronger, expanding the capacity of working memory. As memory capacity expands so does intellective capacity and the student's ability to do higher order tasks.

The Cultural Connection

Now that we have covered the brain's steps for processing, let's turn our attention to understanding how to use culture to help students move through each stage. Culturally responsive information processing techniques grow out of the learning traditions of oral cultures where knowledge is taught and processed through story, song, movement, repetitious chants, rituals, and dialogic talk. They are all forms of elaboration and rely heavily on the brain's memory system.

In response, children's brains create neural pathways in the working memory that are primed for processing information orally and actively. Today, these methods are deeply ingrained in the way learning happens at home for many students of color from community-oriented cultures. If you were to ask their parents to explicitly explain these methods, they'd probably say "That's just the way we did it when I was a kid."

You might think that these traditional cultural learning methods have faded in today's print-heavy and tech-savvy society. Culturally and linguistically diverse families still use them to teach children life skills and to pass along important cultural knowledge from generation to generation. At home and in their communities, traditional learning methods still work. Consequently, culturally and linguistically diverse students come to school with well-developed neural pathways for actively processing information under the right conditions.

Building Intellective Capacity

As a culturally responsive teacher, you should be planning instruction so that students move through the brain's three stages of information processing—input, elaboration, and application. Here I offer four macro level instructional strategies that help move students through each stage. These four strategies should become a staple of your lesson planning and instruction. Within each strategy are a variety of culturally responsive techniques to use. The four macro level instructional strategies are as follows:

- Ignite—Getting the brain's attention
- Chunk—Making information digestible
- Chew—Actively processing new information
- Review—Having a chance to apply new learning

Ignite: Cue the Brain to Pay Attention

Attention is the first step in learning. During the input stage of learning, the brain has to let in the new content. First we have to pay attention. We cannot learn, remember, or understand what we don't first give our attention to. Note that beginning a lesson by simply announcing that you are going to start the lesson will not activate the brain's learning apparatus. Culturally oriented attention-getting strategies focus on waking up students' RAS because that is what happens at home or in the community. This is why in oral cultural traditions, learning or storytelling is started with some attention-getting activity—drumming, chanting, music, hand clapping.

For example, in most African Caribbean, Latin Caribbean, and southern African American cultural circles such as the Gullah Islands off the coast of South Carolina, storytelling traditions have a performance element to them. The "Crick Crack" storytelling chant is an example of this. It looks a little different in various Caribbean countries but has common elements. It is a group performance in which the "audience" participates and there is a close connection between the storyteller and audience to the extent that the two almost become one.

It has the African format of a leader and chorus (in which the participants are both chorus and audience). The "leader" announces that a story is about to be told by calling out "Crick!" The audience responds by shouting back "Crack!" completing the signal that storytelling is about to begin. Then, playfully, the leader tests the audience with riddles to which they may shout out the answers at random (like Hollie's *Jump In* strategy). After this back and forth, the story is told. Through this simple storytelling feature, the RAS is guaranteed to be activated. Use novelty (put on a costume, recite a poem), curiosity (offer a puzzle that can only be put together based on information in the lesson or a mystery to be solved CSI style), or relevance (an emotionally charged headline that turns conventional thinking on its head) to generate excitement and attention.

Other culturally oriented techniques include the following:

Call and Response. Develop a simple back and forth chant that cues the brain that something in particular is going to happen. The brain's neurons start to get excited. The "call" from the teacher that begins the process alerts the student's brain that something is about to happen. The brain becomes curious and begins to pay attention in a different way. The call part of call and response triggers the student's RAS. This is why call and response is done in a lively, energetic way. It activates our RAS and helps us generate mental energy and focus. The takeaway here is to ritualize how you activate students' RAS to turn on their attention.

Music. I remember every Saturday when growing up after breakfast, my mother would put on an upbeat Aretha Franklin record and crank up the volume a bit. That was our cue that it was chore time. Music is a common multicultural attention-getting cue. Find a short upbeat clip and use it to signal the start of some specific type of learning. Maybe it's The Jackson 5's "ABC" to signal time for literacy block. Select a grade appropriate clip.

Provocations. Select an eye-opening quote with strong emotion, a challenging puzzle, or an outrageous statement; create a slideshow with powerful images related to the lesson; or show a video clip that arouses emotions. Challenge dominant culture's worldview or speak to relevant community issues. These types of openings provoke us and create a gentle disequilibrium. These cues not only signal the brain to pay attention but also provide some type of priming that makes the RAS scan the lesson, reading, or discussion for the answer. Wake up the RAS by reading a quote or offering the puzzle from the back of the room. Catch them off guard to increase the impact.

Talk. Create a short, intense, and semistructured talk activity that allows students to engage in culturally congruent ways—overlapping speaking, all at once, or pair share. Give each student a slip of paper with a quote or word. For example, have students share their quote or word and the connection they make to it with another student. Then they swap quotes and find another person to share it as they move around the room.

Remember, the goal of the cueing isn't simple engagement but engagement so that the brain pays attention, recognizes what's coming is important, and lets in the new content being offered. Music, rhythm, and orality are often used as "calls to action" that signal a shift in attention. Find a variety of methods that work for your teaching style and personality. Don't do call and response if it feels uncomfortable to you. If you do, students will sense it and see it as a gimmick, not an authentic way to begin the learning process.

Design the day's lesson to begin by actively activating students' attention. Think about how you will trigger the RAS at the beginning of learning. This type of brain activation doesn't have to be time consuming and should last only 5–10 minutes. If these strategies seem a bit dramatic, they are intended to be. In oral cultures, there is a reliance on oral expression to carry meaning and feelings through its emotional vitality. The goal is to express aliveness and animation to stimulate the senses, just what the RAS likes.

Chunk: Feed the Brain Right-Sized Pieces of Information

Oral cultures rely heavily on the memory system for learning, especially the working memory. But the brain can only hold a certain amount of information for processing at a time. To make the first part of information processing manageable, feed students "right-sized" bits of information. We commonly call this chunking, presenting new information in small, digestible bites. The rule of thumb is 7 + 1. (That's why phone numbers are seven digits.) It is still important that they get the big picture when introducing new concepts or processing, but when teaching for understanding they need smaller chunks of information so that they can easily begin connecting to their current funds of knowledge.

Chew: Help the Brain Process the Content

Next, you will want to help dependent learners "chew on" or process the chunk of content they just received. There are two parts to the chew strategy: unstructured think time and cognitive routines. Begin with unstructured think time as the simplest way to get students to begin processing the content. Why? The brain naturally pushes its mental pause button once it's reached capacity in working memory. Think of a self-operated coin counting machine. It has you feed your bag of loose coins into the slot. At a certain point, the screen flashes a message: Stop and Wait While Processing. It is trying to process the coins it already has and doesn't want to take in more until it has made room.

Our brains work in a similar way. When our working memory's functional capacity is full, the brain cycles down. Remember, in a 40-minute class, the brain takes in information for 12–20 minutes before it cycles down for about 5–10 minutes in order to process what it just took in (Sousa, 2001). The culturally responsive teacher understands both the advantages and limits of the working memory and chunks information so that it fits into the brain's natural processing capacity and uses the down time to allow students to "chew on" what they have just taken in to start the processing cycle. Too often, we continue lecturing without providing time and space for students to do active processing. Dependent learners need the cognitive space to process.

Ramit Mureta, a tenth grade social studies teacher at a large urban high school was openly skeptical when I introduced this strategy at a seminar on culturally responsive information processing. I asked him and his colleagues to go back into their classrooms and simply insert some "chew time" after 15–20 minutes of instruction in the form of a 5–7 minute break. During that break time students processed what they heard, either with a drawing, in writing with the prompt, *"What was the muddiest point you are trying to make sense of?"*, or they could do the Three on a Pencil protocol where students could talk through what they heard. Teachers had to do some front-loading in the beginning to explain the process to students and share the different ways to process.

We came back together three weeks later in a follow-up professional development session to debrief how it went. Ramit's hand was the first to go up. He said he was amazed at how much more his students not only retained from the lesson but how much deeper their understanding was of the content, although he did admit it felt a bit chaotic when he first started using the strategy. That soon passed as students saw the benefit of extra processing time.

Cognitive Routines Aid Elaboration

In addition to giving students unstructured think time, introduce them to cognitive routines for deeper processing. Giving students the chance to actively process information is at the heart of culturally responsive teaching because all new content that makes it to our working memory must be mixed with our existing background knowledge. You become the mediator that helps students make the connection between what they know and how this new information connects to it.

The ultimate goal of culturally responsive instruction is to help students build inside their heads a "cognitive power plant" that allows them to do more complex and challenging work by building on their cultural ways of learning through the explicit focus on *cognitive routines*. These routines are the engines of information processing. When students couple

Figure 8.1 What Are Cognitive Routines?

To do effective information processing, students have to have a way to turn inert information into useable knowledge. Cognitive routines are the basic mental maneuvers the learner uses for information processing, especially when doing higher order thinking and creative problem solving.
Cognitive routines involve the following:

- A sequence of internal learning moves during the elaboration phase of information processing
- The specific structures and protocols a student uses in his sequence of learning moves
- A set of steps students use collectively in the classroom during discussion, brainstorming, group problem solving, Socratic seminar, or other academic conversations

These routines become the cognitive tools the learner uses every time he takes on a learning task.

metacognitive or self-regulation strategies with structured cognitive routines, they are able to monitor and evaluate their comprehension. The ability to identify and utilize cognitive routines is a necessary skill for an independent learner.

As part of the cognitive routine, have students ask these four questions:

- How is this new material connected to what I already know?
- What are the natural relationships and patterns in the material?
- How does it fit together? What larger system is it part of?
- Whose point of view does it represent?

These questions represent the fundamental ways that we process information as the brain goes through the elaboration stage. Cognitive routines as part of a chew strategy give dependent learners a set of explicit learning moves when confronted with new content. There are four key cognitive routines the brain gravitates to when we place new information on working memory's tabletop. Some also call them "thinking dispositions" or "thinking routines" (Cabrera & Colosi, 2012; Ritchhart, 2002). They are:

- *Similarities and Differences.* The brain looks for distinctions between this new information and other similar types of objects, concepts, or events. The brain tries to understand what features make them the same or different.
- *Whole-to-Part.* The brain tries to understand how things are organizing into a system. Is the object, concept, or event part of a larger

system or pattern? Is it a smaller part of the whole or is the whole made up of smaller parts?

- *Relationships*. The brain tries to see the relationship of the object, concept, or event to other things. It wants to understand how it is connected and the role it plays as it interacts with other events, objects, or concepts.
- *Perspectives*. The brain tries to figure out the point of view or perspective being presented. It tries to determine who is telling the story or controlling the narrative.

In the process of carrying out these routines, the brain responds by growing dendrites, creating new neural pathways, and expanding intellective capacity. Remember that cognitive routines aren't really strategies but more like habits of mind. We want to make the routine part of a cognitive habit loop that, over time and with repeated use, becomes automatic for the student. This automaticity is the advantage independent learners have over dependent learners.

Two things are necessary for thinking routines to take hold as cognitive habits:

1. There has to be a strong cue that prompts the thinker into starting the routine.

2. The routine has to be internalized, meaning the learner has to remember the steps in the routine on his own eventually.

That means first you have to scaffold dependent learners into the habit of using them with explicit scaffolding then removing the scaffolds piece by piece, creating some opportunity for productive struggle as the student learns to prompt himself. We call this process *internalization*. It is at this point that culturally responsive teachers need to remember the social-emotional aspects of learning. Struggling of any kind can trigger an amygdala hijack. Students might react with resistance or withdrawal. In your role as their ally, you can help them stay calm and focused as they develop these new habits.

In addition to cognitive routines, here are other techniques to help students "chew on" content for active processing.

Talk to Learn. Learning theorist, Leo Vygotsky (1978) said language is the medium by which children acquire their information. Through informal and formal conversations with other community members, students also acquire the "mental tools" for processing information. Bandura (2001) points out that learning is a sociocultural act governed by language. We learn best when we are able to talk through our cognitive routine. Talking to learn, also called *dialogic talk*, is deeply rooted in oral cultural tradition. This kind of talk gives us the opportunity to organize our thinking into coherent utterances, hear how our thinking sounds out loud, listen to how others respond, and, often, hear others add to or expand on our thinking. Tharp and Gallimore (1991) call this **instructional conversation**, the kind of talk that acts like a mental blender, mixing together new material with existing knowledge in a student's schema.

Using discussion protocols like World Café, Four on a Pencil, and Give One Get One help create variety in the ways students talk to each other in the classroom, offering a chance to both work collaboratively and have their individual voices heard.

Rhythmic Mnemonics in Song or Spoken Word Poetry. Have students write their own songs, raps, or spoken word pieces in the style of the alphabet song or the Schoolhouse Rock! episodes. Music is an important element in oral traditions. When we process new content with music and rhyme, the brain creates multiple neural pathways in different parts of the brain that become permanently connected. This connection across modalities helps strengthen memory. The neurons wire and fire together. Once this wiring happens, the music becomes a cue for remembering key concepts or rules. It's the reason we remember the alphabet song after all these years.

Spoken word is a broad term often applied to performance-style poetry that mixes social awareness, music, and language. Storytelling, spoken word, and poetry slams all fit under this category. Spoken word topics can cover large sociopolitical themes that lend themselves to the cognitive routines such as perspective taking: Love, Racism, Hometown Pride, Politics, and Self-Realization in the context of the curriculum. The world of spoken word is vibrant, compelling, and highly academic in approach. Poetry Slam is essentially a form of competitive performance poetry. Individuals or teams prepare work on a given theme that they perform before judges and an audience. The process of writing, drafting, editing, and rehearsal is vital to the end product, and Slams tend to be very powerful expressions of ideas and feelings through the medium of very skilled writing and performance.

"Story-ify" the Content. Verbal expressiveness is a central cultural theme in oral cultural traditions (Cazden, 2001; Ladson-Billings, 2009). Stories are a mainstay in African American and Latino cultures. Middle Eastern and Southeast Asian communities also have long oral traditions with rich stories. It turns out the brain is wired for stories. Why? When we are being told a story or are telling it, the brain's neurons light up not only in the language processing parts of the brain but in other regions just as if we were performing the action ourselves. For example, if someone in the story is running or jumping, the motor regions of our brain light up. The narrative format lets the brain take big ideas, abstract concepts, and dry facts and transforms them into something we can more easily remember.

As a way to process new content in any subject area, let students weave it together in story form. The Heath Brothers in *Made to Stick* (2007) remind us that the story format makes ideas and concepts "sticky," meaning our brains remember it long after we have heard the story. You can scaffold students into the process by providing the key ideas, words, or concepts from a unit and asking them to weave them together in a coherent, cogent narrative. "Story-ifying" will help students work through the four cognitive routines: *identifying similarities and differences, finding relationships, noticing how things fit together whole-to-part in a system,* and *recognizing point of view.*

Recursive Graphic Organizers, Infographics, and Other Nonlinguistic Representations. Marzano (2004) says that creating pictures, visuals, or other nonlinguistic representations is one of the most powerful ways to process information. According to research, knowledge is stored in two forms: linguistic and visual. Recently, neuroscience has confirmed that the use of nonlinguistic representations increases brain activity and aids information processing. Drawing pictures, flowcharts, or any type of visual is consistent with culturally responsive ways to process information. Incorporate words and images using symbols to represent relationships. Use physical models to represent information.

A common tool that can be used in a culturally responsive way is the graphic organizer. Most teachers use them mainly to activate prior knowledge but students rarely go back to revise them. Use the graphic organizer throughout the lesson. Have students fill it in before the lesson, conduct the lesson, and then ask them to go back and update their graphic organizer with new information they just learned using a different colored pencil or marker. The interaction with the visual representation of information helps speed processing. Have students swap papers with a neighbor or get together in helping trios and compare what is different or the same on their organizers.

Infographics have become a very popular way to graphically display information. Have students create an infographic as a way to process conceptual information or represent their understanding of similarities and differences, relationships between events, concepts, or objects.

Metaphors and Analogies. Information processing through the creation of metaphors and analogies helps by making meaningful connections more obvious. Students use the tools of metaphor building and analogy creation (Wormeli, 2009) to make implicit relationships explicit. The explicit comparisons in a metaphor help students move beyond memorization to deeper comprehension. Resist giving students "plug and play" templates to complete like this: _____ is to _____ as _____ is to _____. This type of frame doesn't build dendrites because students don't really have to grapple with the potential relationships. Instead, have students mine their own funds of knowledge for possible comparisons.

Word Play and Humor. Capitalize on youth culture's rich word play. Word play is deeply rooted in African American culture and has found its way into the mainstream youth culture in the form of urban slang and hip hop. Provide students with opportunities to use word play to process information. Consider setting up "verbal battles" similar to the DJ battles common in hip hop that grew out of the tradition of "playing the dozens." Playing the Dozens is an African American custom of verbal sparring in which two competitors go head to head in a competition of comedic "trash talk" while the audience watches and cheers them on. The Dozens evolved from an oral tradition rooted in West African cultures. It is a contest of personal power—of wit, verbal ability, and mental agility. A skilled contender, win or lose, may gain the respect of the audience. What makes the Dozens a powerful, albeit unique, elaboration tool is that it forces the participants to recognize implicit relationships. Rather than using it to trash talk each other, select elements from the social studies, language arts, or science lesson and have students write their funny "insults" that use the key concepts, facts, or events from the lesson. Instruct students to keep the "insults" friendly and funny, not hurtful or negative.

Review: To Strengthen New Neural Pathways

For new neural pathways to consolidate, the learner has to apply their new understanding within 24 hours. Application can take the form of authentic practice that lets the learner rehearse using his new understanding and correct any misconceptions or weakness in understanding. In *Brain Rules*, Medina (2008) reminds us that rehearsal (using the new knowledge or skill) and repetition (revisiting it) in timed intervals is the mental glue that cements learning. This is where the saying "use it or lose it" comes from. If you learn something new and do it only once or twice, the dendrite connection is very fragile and can begin to fade. Within

20 minutes, you remember only 60% of what you just learned and within 24 hours, you remember only 30%. But if you practice within 24 hours and then practice again later, you remember 80%. Practice at regular intervals, with intensity and deliberateness, is essential for long-term retention and building understanding. The very process of reviewing newly learned content, practicing new skills, or applying new knowledge stimulates dendrite growth, leading to greater intellective capacity.

Figure 8.2 Dendrite Growth

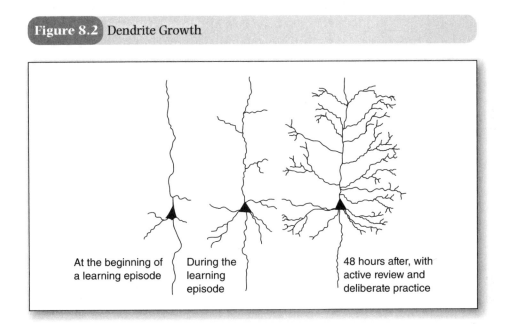

At the beginning of a learning episode During the learning episode 48 hours after, with active review and deliberate practice

Here are some possible ways to help students apply what they have learned.

Play a Game to Review. Games provide a unique opportunity to review and rehearse new knowledge. The very act of playing the game encourages the brain to strengthen the new neural pathways by making the learner continuously search his memory for information. Even the brains of those students only watching the game are firing and wiring thanks to mirror neurons.

Try to set up games like Jeopardy, Family Feud, Pyramid, or Pictionary that can be played with teams. Be sure to set up teams so that dependent learners can actively participate and be successful. You might give students some preparation time to review core concepts. These games are particularly helpful because they are set up uniquely. For example, Jeopardy provides the answer. The player has to come up with the question, forcing him to think in terms of relationships, whole-to-part systems, and point of view. These are the basic thinking dispositions that you are trying to cultivate. The game Pyramid has one player read off a list of items. The other player must understand the implicit relationship between them. All these activities help strengthen the fragile neural pathway made up of new dendrite growth. These games help students create well-rehearsed mental routines.

Solve the Mystery or Real-Life Problem. At the start of a unit or lesson, set up a problem or mystery to be solved. Once students have worked through the elaboration stage, have them return to the problem and apply their new knowledge to solve the problem or mystery.

Work on Long-Term Projects*.* Anchor a unit with a place-based learning activity connected to a real life community issue. Once instruction has been delivered, use the project as an opportunity to apply new skills and knowledge. Select a project that addresses a real life task. For example, planning a community garden can be a project to anchor a science unit on soil. Collaborate with local organic farmers or local community gardens in the vicinity of the school.

CULTURALLY RESPONSIVE INFORMATION PROCESSING IN MATH AND SCIENCE

A teacher recently said to me he wasn't convinced about using culturally responsive teaching in math. "Teaching equations is pretty straightforward," he said. "How do you do that without making up some gimmick?"

His comment is pretty typical among math and science teachers I run into, so I thought it was important to address it. Culturally responsive teaching has usually been presented to them as an engagement strategy designed to motivate students. Most often the examples used to demonstrate it are focused on language arts and social studies. We have not made it clear to math and science teachers how they would interject culture into the teaching of math when teaching formulas and procedures seems straightforward and culturally neutral.

The power of culturally responsive teaching is in its ability to help students deepen their understanding of core concepts as well as build automaticity and fluency with core facts. The Common Core State Standards in math actually call for helping all students develop greater conceptual understanding and mathematical thinking, not just on trying to get students faster with procedural skills such as steps for solving an equation. Helping students understand math concepts means helping them not just with procedural knowledge such as how to solve for x but also understanding how this concept is relevant to everyday life.

Using information processing strategies consistent with culturally and linguistically diverse students from oral and collectivist cultures to scaffold deeper conceptual understanding is culturally responsive teaching, without ever having to mention race or culture. Yet, recognizing that problem-based learning that looks at sociopolitical issues relevant to culturally and linguistically diverse students' lives grounds the context of mathematics and science. For example, former classroom teacher Jana Dean (2006) wrote about using issues of rising gas prices in urban areas as an entry point for conceptual understanding of algebra and its application in real life.

Helping students build an academic vocabulary in math and science will lay a strong foundation for doing more rigorous conceptual thinking in those subject areas. This is where culturally responsive information processing techniques are most effective. For example, sixth grade science teacher Janelle Reed admitted she was pretty traditional when it came to vocabulary instruction in science. She knew the academic vocabulary associated with science was important but didn't devote a lot of class time to it. At the beginning of every week, students in her class got a list of science terms and concept words. There would be a test at the end of the week. Once she gave them the list, they were on their own to learn the words. She encouraged them to use the dictionary and write out sentences using the vocabulary. She did a few word study activities, but by the end of the week few students had learned the vocabulary.

She started to rethink her approach after studying culturally oriented information processing methods to build independent learning. She says she'd always thought being culturally responsive meant explicitly tying everything to students' culture or race. Instead, she redesigned her science vocabulary instruction to focus on culturally grounded information processing. Rather than a weekly take-home vocabulary list, she tried using sorting and games in class to help students with learning vocabulary for the week's unit and committing it to their long-term memory. The vocabulary games had students working and processing in new ways. The games she picked emphasized collaboration and teamwork. She says engagement went through the roof. One student said in passing, "Oh, we are learning. You are just hiding it in the fun." All she could do was smile. At the end of the unit, she noticed their conceptual understanding of the lesson was deeper and their class discussions were richer as they used the vocabulary more frequently.

IMPLICATIONS FOR SUPPORTING DEPENDENT LEARNERS AND BUILDING INTELLECTIVE CAPACITY

Helping dependent learners process information more effectively is an important step toward closing the achievement gap. Our goal is to help culturally and linguistically diverse students build in their heads a "cognitive power plant" that will get them ready to take on the rigorous Common Core State Standards at every grade level. Ultimately, we want to empower them by helping them become independent learners who are capable of taking on any academic challenge.

Keep in mind that culturally responsive information processing doesn't have to be race-specific. It does have to be grounded in the context of students' lives. Our task is to find ways to access their funds of knowledge and understand their home-based ways of learning as starting points for designing more authentic learning experiences.

CHAPTER SUMMARY

- Simply adding surface-level cultural details to low-level decontextualized activities doesn't offer any cognitive challenge and won't build intellective capacity.
- Culturally responsive teaching for information processing follows the brain's natural input, elaboration, and application cycle.
- Students need to learn and internalize cognitive routines in order to move toward more independent learning.
- Engagement is a means to an end, not the end goal of culturally responsive teaching.

INVITATION TO INQUIRY

- How do you incorporate information processing into your lessons currently?
- How often do students have a chance to actively work through the elaboration stage of processing?
- How explicitly have you taught students about using a set of cognitive routines to process content? Do you check to ensure they have internalized the routines?
- Where do you see opportunity for incorporating more information processing activities in your instruction?

GOING DEEPER

- *Student Success with Thinking Maps: School-Based Research, Results, and Models for Achievement Using Visual Tools* (2011) by David Hyerle and Larry Alper
- *Making Thinking Visible: How to Promote Engagement, Understanding, and Independence for All Learners* (2011) by Ron Ritchhart, Mark Church, and Karin Morrison
- *Metaphors and Analogies: Power Tools for Teaching Any Subject* (2009) by Rick Wormeli
- *Reading for Their Life: (Re) Building the Textual Lineages of African American Adolescent Males* (2009) by Alfred Tatum
- *Thinking at Every Desk: Four Simple Skills to Transform Your Classroom* (2012) by Derek Cabrera and Laura Colosi

9 Creating a Culturally Responsive Community for Learning

Seeing the Environment as the Second Teacher

Every person needs a place that is furnished with hope.

—Maya Angelou

Children grow into the intellectual life around them.

—Leo Vygotsky

In this chapter, we look at the last practice area of the Ready for Rigor frame: Community of Learners and Learning Environment. We will explore ways that we can build a sense of community and connection in the classroom so that it supports the social, emotional, and intellectual safety of all students of color and English learners, but especially those dependent learners who have yet to create for themselves a strong learner identity and sense of confidence. Routines, aesthetics, talk structures, and task variety are the brick and mortar that build a strong classroom community. If we are going to push dependent learners in positive ways to stretch themselves we have to offer them a safe community to do it in.

In culturally responsive pedagogy, the classroom is a critical container for empowering marginalized students. It serves as a space that reflects the values of trust, partnership, and academic mindset that are at its core.

ETHOS VERSUS ARTIFACTS

In my experience talking with teachers about culturally responsive classrooms, there is a tendency to get stuck on how to decorate the room with the right cultural artifacts rather than how to create the right ethos to set the social and emotional tone (Brown & Campione, 1994; Ladson-Billings, 2009).

We name classrooms after Ivy League universities and colleges, but we need to also attend to the spirit of community in the classroom that allows all students to develop the confidence and ability to take advantage of an Ivy League education. A culturally responsive classroom environment goes beyond decorating the walls with cultural artifacts that highlight the rich history of African Americans, Latinos, or other ethnic groups. It also offers an emotionally stable and responsive environment.

I remember meeting with a colleague who is an instructional coach. She shared a story that highlighted the importance of having an ethos of caring in the classroom. She mentioned that on a recent classroom walk-through with a school principal and a few other visitors, the group walked into an elementary classroom where the teacher was busy presenting the lesson and students were listening and working. On one side of the room was a small Latino boy on the floor crying, not hysterical but just gentle sobbing. No one was tending to him. She said everyone ignored him, even the walk-through group. Many looked and then just kept on going. She said she couldn't take it and went over and gently laid a hand on his back and rubbed for a minute. He stopped and looked at her. No words were exchanged. He sat up and pulled himself together. She rejoined the group as they moved to the next classroom. She said she often wondered what happened to that little boy.

Over coffee, we tried to imagine the atmosphere of that classroom that allowed the little boy to cry alone in the book cove. Classroom structures and processes need to tend to the emotional well-being of everyone rather than just on covering the day's lesson plan.

Bilingual literacy educator, Kris Gutierrez (2008) points out that the classroom is more than just walls to be dressed or a place for desks. It is a sociocultural "third space," a place for students to explore their individual and collective identities through different types of discourse, uses of language, and emotional support. The culturally responsive teacher doesn't approach the classroom environment with a "window dressing" mindset but instead acknowledges that it is a powerful container in its own right that reflects, communicates, and shapes values.

When our neuroceptive mechanisms confirm that our surroundings are physically, socially, and intellectually safe, we go into a state of relaxed alertness and are primed for learning. However, when our senses read the environmental cues as threatening because of a cultural mismatch or subtle microaggressions, the brain goes on alert and triggers stress-producing defensive strategies.

If we want the classroom environment to be a third space, we have to carefully reexamine the elements in the environment that are visual representations of core collectivist values about learning and intellectual character. We must ask ourselves:

- What values do we want to communicate through our environment?
- How do we want children to experience their time in our classroom?
- What do the artifacts on the walls communicate to students, parents, or me about what is important?
- What do we want the environment to "teach" those who are in it?

CLASSROOM AESTHETICS AND SYMBOLS

In many collectivist cultures, beauty and harmony are important values that extend to the environment. An environment that is crowded or cluttered may obscure the values you have in mind. Think carefully about what visuals are displayed on the walls. They send a nonverbal message about what and who is valued in the classroom. Unconsciously, we pick up clues about affirmation and validation from our surroundings. Remember that our RAS continuously scans the environment and takes in millions of bits of information and evaluates it almost instantaneously. Just below consciousness, our brain is determining if there is anything in the environment that creates a sense of well-being based on what we recognize from our home and community environment.

Rather than prepackaged "multicultural" bulletin board cut-outs or standard ethnic "heroes" posters, find authentic cultural elements that add real value to the classroom:

- Purchase inexpensive prints to hang of contemporary and traditional artists representing cultures in your classroom.

- Establish an "artwork on loan" program where parents "loan" the classroom their artwork for a period of time.
- Use colors or artistic styles representing students' culture as a visual backdrop on bulletin boards year round. Incorporate them into art activities.
- Bring in photographs of murals and other community art into the classroom. Partner with local art organizations to get access to interesting photos.
- Decorate with authentic textiles and handcrafts as accents not "artifacts."
- Include naturalistic elements signifying nature (air, earth, water, and fire).
- Post diagrams of patents from engineers and inventors of color.

Remember that the signs and symbols around us communicate with our collective unconscious mind. Think about the cultural values of your students and translate those values into concrete objects and symbols that you can display or integrate into the classroom. Use the worksheet below to brainstorm how you might select meaningful artifacts and cultural symbols for display in the classroom.

Figure 9.1 Classroom Design

Cultural Value	Possible Symbols and Artifacts
Example: *Collective work and responsibility*	*Posters of social movements, especially with youth—Freedom Riders, community gardens in urban areas*

Routines and Rituals

Routines

We usually talk about routines as a method for classroom management. In the culturally responsive classroom, routines are a way to make space for the important affirming/communal activities that create social bonds among students. Over time, routines become invisible and part of the classroom culture that help create a positive energy and the classroom's ethos.

When routines and procedures are carefully taught, modeled, and established in the classroom, children know what's expected of them and how to do certain things on their own. Having these predictable patterns in place allows teachers to spend more time in meaningful instruction and aids social cooperation in the classroom. Whatever the focus of your classroom, think about the climate you'd like to create.

What makes the routines culturally responsive is the focus on one or more of the key collectivist values. Design common routines to emphasize interdependency and social connection.

Here are some ideas for how to reimagine routines that are culturally responsive.

- Open the day with a centering activity versus a traditional morning meeting.
- Use music or call and response to facilitate transitions from one activity to another.
- Create after lunch transition routines to help students get their heads back into schoolwork.
- Create routines for "parallel" independent work or sponge or anchor activities.

Before establishing specific procedures or routines, it is necessary to talk with students about why routines are important and to review key procedures. During this discussion, you should be able to talk about the rationale behind various routines that connect to what is important to students. When possible, invite students to create procedures with you. This process can nurture a sense of ownership and community in your classroom. Ensure that students understand the reason for the routine. Remember that it will probably be necessary to revisit this process as you see the need.

Rituals

The ethos in the classroom has to support students to adopt a positive academic mindset. Rituals as part of the classroom culture help combine emotional vitality and spiritually, two core values in collectivist cultures.

As a culturally responsive educator, look for opportunities to ignite students' spirits and emotions. The branch of neuroscience called "contemplative neuroscience" helps us understand the power of rituals. With the repetition of ritual, the brain learns to associate sensory experiences—the sounds, smells, and feelings of ceremony—with the spiritual practice. Once those links are formed, sensory cues can bring us back to a contemplative state very powerfully and quickly. Thus, the soft, high voices of a choir, the burning incense, the murmur of parishioners all become signals that trigger our feeling of openness to the divine (Hanson, 2013).

While we may not be trying to invoke the divine in the classroom, rituals can reinforce inspiration, affirmation, and validation for students. These rituals can help reinforce elements of academic mindset such as "I belong" or "I can do this." Rituals can reinforce the behaviors we want, create focus and a sense of belonging, and make change stick.

Another major benefit of established rituals and routines is that they capitalize on our brains' ability to put desirable behaviors on autopilot, allowing us to reach our goals even when we are distracted or preoccupied with other things. Here are some ideas for classroom rituals for affirmation and validation.

- ***Institute the morning recitation of common poem or verse.*** A common verse that expresses important values or ideas can build a sense of shared mission. A small community school serving mostly Latino and Cambodian families in Oakland begins each day with the reading of the school's "head, heart, and hands" verse. Every classroom begins the day with the communal reading of the verse in English, then Spanish, and then Khmer.

- ***As a class, watch and respond to short, inspiring TED (Technology, Entertainment, and Design) talks or uplifting poetry,*** quotes, or songs that affirm common cultural values, validate students' experiences, or reinforce an academic mindset. Sing freedom songs ("Sweet Honey in the Rock"), traditional cultural songs, or uplifting pop songs such as "I Believe I Can Fly" or "Hall of Fame." They can serve as a class anthem. Rework lyrics of popular songs. English teacher Linda Christensen (2009) says she sometimes starts class with students' original poetry or a selection that has personal meaning. She says poetry quickly brings students' voices into the center of the classroom community.

    Over the years, I have learned that sometimes writing a poem or interior monologue from history or literature can create a space in the classroom for a different way of knowing, a different way of expressing knowledge about a fictional character or a historical decision. My skin, my blood, my bones understand events before my mind catches up and processes the information.

Too often, learning becomes recitation, the dull retelling of facts, but writing poetry helps unleash sorrow or joy, the human understanding of loss and creation across cultures, centuries, and continents, so I try to create opportunities for students to demonstrate their knowledge through poetry and interior monologues. (p. 50)

- ***Share and reflect on community wisdom***. Ask parents for "dichos" (proverbs and sayings) they use at home or grew up with. Proverbs that guide and impart knowledge are found in all cultures but carry a lot of weight in oral cultures that rely on them to transmit cultural knowledge. These pithy sayings express universal truths in just a few words and are easily remembered. They strengthen our ties to our own culture by reminding us where we came from. Write them down and post them around the classroom.
- ***Begin a new unit with the reading of quotes*** or short excerpts of relevant narratives.

Brainstorm with colleagues to develop other unique rituals to support your students given their age and grade level.

STUDENT AGENCY AND VOICE

One of the primary ways students develop a sense of agency and independence is through language and talk. Talking helps us process our learning. Talking helps us connect with others. Talking helps us expand our thinking when we hear the ideas of others. Vygotsky refers to this as the sociocultural nature of learning. We learn more when we are in conversation with others. Yet the traditional talk structures in most classrooms revolve around a *passive-receptive* style, meaning students are passive listeners and most discourse is centered around "teacher talk." Teachers dominate the air space in most classrooms. When students are allowed to talk, it is in this orderly, turn-taking way that doesn't resemble the way most culturally and linguistically diverse students engage in discourse outside of school or at home.

The classroom has to be designed around talk and task structures that allow students to define the people they see themselves becoming. Simply calling students "scholars" or telling them they are smart is not enough to shape their internal identity. When students have a chance to narrate their lives, put language to their experience, and process their thinking through discourse they begin to notice and name their own competence.

In collectivist cultures, the primary way we name and notice is through a variety of talk structures, each with its own situational appropriateness. As you create a learning culture in your classroom, consider how you will include social and academic talk structures.

Social Talk Structures

Consider culturally responsive talk structures that are more participatory and interactive. Culturally oriented speakers expect listeners to engage them actively through vocalization, motion, or movement as they are speaking. Students are used to this discourse pattern at home and in their community. In addition to this back and forth nature of talk, culturally and linguistically diverse students participate in what is called "cooperative overlapping," recognizable by the way students jump in when someone else is talking and begins talking. It isn't considered rude but a highly social talk structure. It's also called rapport-talk because it is a communication pattern used to build community. We see it at social get-togethers as people flow in and out of small group conversations.

Allow space for rapport-talk as a warm up to a lesson or unit. In addition to this type of social talk, consider also incorporating less traditional tools such as digital storytelling that allow students to share issues important to them. At the other end of the spectrum are dyads—a discourse structure that gives each speaker equal time to talk and space to be heard, uninterrupted. There are other types of social talk structures to draw from. The point here is to create variety in the talk structures students encounter in the classroom. If you are new to different communication patterns, it may take a while to get used to the higher noise level. You might experience it as chaotic. This is where we get to practice widening our cultural aperture.

Academic Talk Structures

One of the most important tools for a culturally responsive teacher is **instructional conversation**. The ability to form, express, and exchange ideas is best taught through dialogue, questioning, and the sharing of ideas. Instructional conversation provides the space to do this type of processing. It shouldn't be confused with Socratic seminars or similar instructional tools. Instructional conversation is focused on giving students language to talk about their own learning and thinking process. There are a variety of tools you can use to provide flexible scaffolding without rigid structure to help dependent learners build their capacity and stamina to engage in meaningful academic dialogue.

Zwiers and Crawford (2011), in *Academic Conversations*, point out that in many classrooms, talking activities are used in limited ways that lead to interaction without depth—quick think-pair-share or turn and talks routinely break up a long activity. Even with more time, these talk activities quickly lose focus because students lack the skills to stay on topic or extend it. Instead, they suggest we equip students with collaborative protocols that help instructional conversation lead to deeper learning. The National School Reform Faculty (NSRF) provides teachers in professional learning communities with protocols to support their instructional conversations. They have modified their protocols for use in elementary and middle school classrooms. These protocols help build equity of participation understanding of a concept from basic to higher order as well as develop active listening skills. Here are three powerful protocols easily incorporated into elementary or secondary classrooms to scaffold instructional conversation.

- **Helping Trios**: Each student presents something they are working on and get help from classmates.
- **Chalk Talk**: Using markers and a one large sheet of butcher paper, in silence students write responses to an essential question related to a unit or lesson. Students are able to build on other ideas written.
- **World Café**: Students rotate through tables discussing an essential question and recording parts of their conversation.

IMPLICATIONS FOR SUPPORTING DEPENDENT LEARNERS AND BUILDING INTELLECTIVE CAPACITY

We should not underestimate the power of the classroom community to support dependent learners' move toward more independent learning. The feeling, tone, and structure of a welcoming classroom can help students enter and maintain a state of relaxed alertness that lays the foundation for authentic engagement.

In addition to the social-emotional aspects of classroom culture, routines and rituals help reinforce students' cognitive development by instilling a sense of order and process.

CHAPTER SUMMARY

- The classroom environment is an important element in culturally responsive teaching.
- The goal is to create not just an aesthetically pleasing environment but a strong ethos or feeling tone as well.
- Routines and rituals help reflect collectivist cultural values as well as support deeper learning.
- Students need regular opportunities to share their views and opinions about how the classroom culture and community is developed.

INVITATION TO INQUIRY

- What are the different talk structures in your classroom?
- What routines and rituals are in operation? What do they accomplish? Are they aligned with cultural practices significant to your students?
- How would you characterize the ethos in the classroom? How do you know? How do you think students would describe it?

GOING DEEPER

- *Classroom Discourse: The Language of Teaching and Learning* (2001) by Courtney B. Cazden
- *Academic Conversations: Classroom Talk That Fosters Critical Thinking and Content Understandings* (2011) by Jeff Zwiers & Marie Crawford
- *The Power of Protocols: An Educator's Guide to Better Practice*, 3rd edition (2013) by Joseph P. McDonald, Nancy Mohr, Alan Dichter, and Elizabeth C. McDonald

Epilogue

Better is possible. It does not take genius. It takes diligence. It takes moral clarity. It takes ingenuity. And above all, it takes a willingness to try.

—Atul Gawande, Surgeon and Author,
Better: A Surgeon's Notes on Performance

Leadership means taking responsibility for what matters to you.

—National Equity Project

A few final thoughts: The problem of the achievement gap won't be solved by simply trying to motivate students of color to become more engaged learners. We have to focus on two-tiered learning: What are the strategies we can use to help dependent learners do complex thinking, and how do we build our own teaching practice in order to help them. We have to create school environments that welcome their natural ways of learning and shape content so that they see its connection to their lives and funds of knowledge.

Sunday Afternoon Moves

The question we usually have at this point is: So, now what? What do we do tomorrow? Teachers always talk about professional learning in terms of how well information passes the Monday Morning test: Can I walk into my classroom on Monday morning and start using what I have just learned? Some of you might even feel frustrated that I didn't give you a step-by-step how-to guide for creating culturally responsive lessons.

I want to offer you a reframe. Rather than focus on your Monday morning moves, think about your Sunday afternoon planning, that level of curriculum design and lesson planning that happens before you step back into the classroom at the start of the week.

- Rethink how you will organize time in your classroom to accommodate more information processing time, opportunities for formative assessments that provide some cognitive insight, and instructional conversation to share wise feedback.
- Revisit your lesson plans and begin to analyze and deconstruct them for culturally responsive elements shared in the book.
- Begin to write out your lesson plans if you haven't made that a regular part of your practice so that you can refine your instructional "recipe" for building students' capacity to be independent learners.
- Pick one small thing from each of the four areas of the Ready for Rigor frame and begin working them into your daily practice.

Embracing Conscious Incompetence

As you begin refining your teaching practice, be prepared to embrace your conscious incompetence, that awareness and awkwardness that comes with trying out something new. Education change expert, Michael Fullan calls this the "implementation dip"—that inevitable bumpiness, self-consciousness, and feeling of chaos that comes up when you are trying a new skill or practice and before it becomes automatic. In *Leading in a Culture of Change* (2007), Fullan points out that any innovation worth its salt calls on people to go through this process. Remember that even as educators, we are subjected to the same amygdala hijack as our students. We feel anxious, fearful, confused, and overwhelmed as we step outside our comfort zone. Embrace this stage and use it as a time for inquiry and reflection because this too shall pass.

A note to school leaders: Just as teachers have to create safe spaces for students to try new learning moves, school leaders have to create safe spaces for teachers to expand their instructional repertoire to be more culturally responsive. Our teacher support and evaluation processes have to create allowances for innovation and not penalize teachers for those brief periods of chaos that come with innovation.

Leading for Equity

As a skilled, culturally responsive educator, you are uniquely positioned to be a leader for equity. Leadership doesn't always mean being out in front of a group. Instead, it can mean leading by example and as part of a group of concerned educators working for change. Here are some simple suggestions:

- Open your classroom door to share new ideas and practices.
- Participate in school-level inquiry to question unproductive practices.
- Work on creating positive relationships with students' families so that you are in partnership with them in a new way.
- Look at the data and strategize ways to reduce the predictability of who succeeds and who fails in your classroom based on race, gender, class, or language. Then begin engaging others at the school level to do the same.
- Interrupt instructional practices that produce dependent learners or keep them stuck. Instead focus on including more culturally responsive techniques that build brain power while affirming and validating. Document student results and go public with what you learned.
- Build your will, skill, and capacity to engage in "courageous conversations" about race, implicit bias, and structural racialization that limit the learning opportunities for culturally and linguistically diverse students. Help other teachers shift from deficit-focused language to asset-based discourse.

We all know that we can do better in running schools so that they are learning organizations that support teachers' professional learning and students' social, emotional, and cognitive development in culturally supportive ways. The trick is moving from just complaining about issues that are beyond our control to becoming excellent at raising the achievement of students of color that are right in front of us. If you do, you will expand your influence. You will create a platform that allows you the chance to address issues of policy and equity on behalf of all students and their families.

Glossary

The definitions in this glossary are offered in everyday language as much as possible to help deepen your understanding of key concepts in neuroscience and culturally responsive teaching.

Affirmation. The practice of intentionally noticing and admiring the uniqueness of culturally and linguistically diverse students. It includes seeing as positive those elements that the dominant culture tries to portray as unattractive or undesirable, such as their hair, skin color, verbal agility, or energetic style.

Alliance. It is the second part of the learning partnership equation. Alliance focuses on helping the dependent learner begin and stay on the arduous path toward independent learning. An alliance is more than a friendship. It is a relationship of mutual support as partners navigate through challenging situations.

Amygdala hijack. The process when the amygdala is in an active state of stress, fear, or anxiety. It signals the body to release the stress hormone, cortisol. The cortisol blocks rational thinking and temporarily reduces the capacity of the working memory making learning difficult.

Autonomic nervous system. This is the portion of the nervous system comprised of the spinal cord and brain. It includes the sympathetic nervous system, parasympathetic nervous system, and polyvagal nervous system.

Cognitive insight. It is the third part of the learning partnership. It is the teacher's ability to understand a student's internal learning process. Formative assessments and instructional conversation are key tools for gaining insight into a student's learning moves.

Cortisol. Cortisol is the primary stress hormone. Chronic exposure to cortisol because of stress reduces working memory and suppresses the body's immune system.

Cultural archetype. It is a similar set of beliefs, values, or behaviors that show up in different cultures.

Culturally responsive teaching. The process of using familiar cultural information and processes to scaffold learning. Emphasizes communal orientation. Focused on relationships, cognitive scaffolding, and critical social awareness.

Dendrites. Treelike extensions at the beginning of a neuron that help increase its surface area. These tiny tentacles receive information from other neurons and transmit electrical stimulation. Dendrites grow in response to learning, especially a challenging task. The more dendrites the neuron generates the more brainpower it creates.

Dopamine. A chemical in the brain associated with attention and reward-stimulated learning. Our brains release dopamine when we are playing, laughing, exercising, and receiving acknowledgment (e.g., praise) for achievement.

Fixed mindset. Fixed mindset students believe their basic abilities, their intelligence, and their talents are just fixed traits. For high achievers, their goal becomes to look smart all the time and never risk looking dumb. For low achievers, their goal is to avoid challenging work so as not to confirm their low intelligence.

Formative assessments. Also called assessment *for* learning. It is the process of using simple tools to determine how well content has been learned so that the learner can make adjustments to his learning moves in the moment.

Gray matter. Gray matter refers to the brownish-gray color of the nerve cell bodies (neurons). The wrinkled appearance of the brain results from the overgrowth of gray matter in the small skull cavity.

Growth mindset. In a growth mindset, students understand that their talents and abilities can be developed through effort, active learning, and persistence.

Implicit bias. Refers to the unconscious attitudes and stereotypes that shape our responses to certain groups especially around race, class, and language. Implicit bias operates involuntarily, often without one's aware-ness or intentional control. Implicit bias is not implicit racism.

Information processing. The brain's process of turning inert facts and content into useable knowledge. Includes three stages: input, elaboration, and application. Active information processing stimulates brain growth.

Instructional conversation. Classroom discourse that is focused on having students talk about their learning process and learning moves. It is an extension of information processing and feedback.

Intellective capacity. Refers to a student's malleable information processing power. Also called fluid intelligence or intellectual competence. Intellective capacity grows through neuroplasticity.

Internalized oppression. When people are targeted, discriminated against, or oppressed over a period of time, they often internalize (believe and make part of their internal view of themselves) the myths and misinformation that society holds about their group.

Learned helplessness. The victim mentality a learner adopts when repeatedly subjected to negative stimulus. Over time the learner stops trying to avoid the stimulus and believes he is helpless to change the situation. Includes a lack of confidence in one's ability and a belief that effort is useless.

Learning partnership. A learning partnership is a teacher-student relationship in which the teacher builds trust and becomes the student's ally in order to help the student reach a higher level of achievement.

Limbic region. The limbic is the second brain layer. Also called the mammalian brain. It is involved in regulation of emotion, memory, and processing complex socioemotional communication. The amygdala is located here.

Long-term memory. Long-term memory is created when short-term memory is strengthened through review and meaningful association with existing funds of knowledge. This strengthening results in a physical change in the structure of neuronal circuits, creating more gray matter in the brain.

Mental model. A mental model is an explanation of someone's thought process about how something works in the real world. It is one's internal representation of the surrounding world. Mental models shape our behavior, decision making, and relating to others. See also Schema.

Microaggressions. They are small, subtle verbal insults or nonverbal actions directed at people of color that intentionally or unintentionally communicate mistrust or hostility, such as clutching one's purse if a person of color gets into an elevator or when store personnel follow a person of color around a store while he is shopping.

Mindset. A set of mental attitudes that determines how one will interpret and respond to situations. See also Fixed mindset and Growth mindset.

Myelin. The fatty substance that covers and protects nerves. Myelin acts like a conductor in an electrical system, ensuring that messages sent along the neuron are not lost as they travel to the next neuron. Myelin enhances the function of neurons and dendrites.

Myelination. The formation of the myelin sheath around the body of a neuron to increase the speed of electrical impulses containing information.

Negativity bias. The brain's innate tendency to pay more attention to and overreact to negative events, information, and experiences. Believed to be part of the stereotyping feature of our safety-threat system charged with keeping us safe.

Neocortex region. It is the newest layer of the brain. Also called the pre-frontal cortex (PFC). It is the hub of neural networks that directs intake and output to almost all other regions of the brain. Through executive functions in the PFC, the brain moves information to the working memory to be mentally manipulated so it becomes long-term knowledge. This area of the brain also controls conscious decision making, organizing, analyzing, self-monitoring, self-correcting, reflection, and problem solving.

Neuroception. Describes the process our brain uses to distinguish whether situations or people are safe, dangerous, or life threatening. The autonomic nervous system, particularly the polyvagal nerve, is responsible for controlling neuroception. See also Safety-threat detection system.

Neurons. Specialized cells in the brain and throughout the nervous system that control storage and processing of information to, from, and within the brain, spinal cord, and nerves. Neurons are composed of a main cell body, a single major axon for outgoing electrical signals, and a varying number of dendrites to pass along coded information throughout the nervous system.

Neuroplasticity. Refers to the capacity of the brain to change its structure and reorganize itself in response to injury, experience, or challenge. Associated with expanded learning capacity.

Oxytocin. Oxytocin is a neurotransmitter that stimulates our sense of connection with others. It is called the bonding hormone.

Productive struggle. When the learner has developed the necessary strategies for working through something difficult. The mental activity that takes place when students are in their zone of proximal development.

Rapport. A close and harmonious relationship between people characterized by a sense of connection, personal regard, and trust.

Relaxed alertness. It is the optimum learning state of the brain. The brain experiences low threat while it is alert and paying attention with anticipation. The term can also apply to the emotional tone of the classroom that creates a social and intellectually safe environment.

Reticular activating system (RAS). Located in the reptilian region of the brain, it is the portal through which nearly all information enters the brain. (Smells are the exception; they go directly into your brain's emotional area.) It filters all incoming stimuli and decides what to pay attention to and what to ignore. Novelty, curiosity, changes in the environment, surprise, danger, and movement all capture the attention of the RAS. It sends signals to the amygdala when it detects a social or physical threat.

Safety-threat detection system. Our brain's system to help carry out its prime directive: minimize threats and maximize well-being. See also Neuroception.

Schema. A schema is a cognitive framework or concept that helps organize and interpret information. Schemas can be useful because they allow us to take shortcuts in interpreting the vast amount of information that is available in our environment. However, these mental frameworks also cause us to exclude pertinent information to instead focus only on things that confirm our preexisting beliefs and ideas.

Self-efficacy. One's internal belief and self-confidence that one has the power and skills to shape the direction of one's learning experience.

Short-term memory. This stage of memory holds and manipulates information for use only in the immediate future, for approximately one minute, until the RAS decides to let it into the working memory.

Sociopolitical context. A term used to describe the series of mutually reinforcing policies and practices across social, economic, and political domains that contribute to disparities and unequal opportunities for people of color in housing, transportation, education, and health care, to name a few. These unequal opportunities result in unequal outcomes along racial and class lines.

Stereotype threat. Refers to a student's fear of confirming a negative stereotype about his racial, ethnic, or socioeconomic group (i.e., African Americans aren't smart) by his actions (such as failing a test). This anxiety triggers an amygdala hijack, releasing stress hormones and shutting down all learning, making it more likely that he will fail.

Structural racialization. Refers to the ways in which supposedly race neutral policies and practices across social, political, and economic institutions create racialized outcomes. See also sociopolitical context.

Validation. Refers to the explicit recognition and acknowledgment of historical institutional racism, negative stereotyping, and generalizations that impact culturally and linguistically diverse students.

Warm demander. A teacher who communicates personal warmth toward students while at the same time demands they work toward high standards. Provides concrete guidance and support for meeting the standards, particularly corrective feedback, opportunities for information processing, and culturally relevant meaning making.

Wise feedback. Wise feedback is a way of giving feedback that reassures the student that he is not viewed in light of a negative stereotype. We assume rather than doubt his intellectual abilities. Wise feedback conveys faith in the potential of the student while being honest about where he is right now.

Working memory. The working memory is the area in the brain where new information is coupled with existing knowledge. The elaboration stage of information processing takes place mainly in the working memory.

Zone of proximal development. The difference between what a learner can do without help and what he can do with help. Because learning in the zone of proximal development is a stretch for a student, the brain responds by growing more neurons and dendrites. Also called the ZPD.

References and Further Reading

Alexander, M. (2012). *The new Jim Crow: Mass incarceration in the age of colorblindness.* San Francisco: New Press.

Allington, R., & McGill-Franzen, A. (1989). School response to reading failure: Chapter 1 and special education students in grades 2, 4, & 8. *Elementary School Journal, 89,* 529–542.

Amabile, T., & Kramer, S. (2012). *The progress principle: Using small wins to ignite joy, engagement, and creativity at work.* Cambridge: Harvard Business Review.

Angelou, M. (1994). *The complete collected poems of Maya Angelou.* New York: Random House.

Antrop-González, R., & De Jesús, A. (2006). Toward a theory of critical care in urban small school reform: Examining structures and pedagogies of caring in two Latino community-based schools. *International Journal of Qualitative Studies in Education, 19*(4), 409–433.

Bandura, A. (1986). *Social foundations of thought and action: A social cognitive theory.* Englewood Cliffs, NJ: Prentice Hall.

Bandura, A. (2001). Social cognitive theory: An agentic perspective. *Annual Review of Psychology, 52,* 1–26.

Banks, J. A. (2002). *An introduction to multicultural education.* Boston: Allyn & Bacon.

Berger, R., Rugen, L., & Woodfin, L. (2014). *Leaders of their own learning: Transforming schools through student-engaged assessment.* San Francisco, CA: Jossey-Bass.

Black, P., & William, D. (1998). Inside the black box: Raising standards through classroom assessment. *Phi Delta Kappan, 80,* 139–148.

Bordin, E. (1994). Theory and research on the therapeutic working alliance: New directions. In A. Horvath & L. Greenberg (Eds.), *The working alliance: Theory, research, and practice.* San Francisco: Wiley.

Borman, G., & Overman, L. (2004). Academic resilience among poor and minority students. *Elementary School Journal, 104*(3), 177–195.

Boykin, A. W. (2000). The talent development model of schooling: Placing students at promise for academic success. *Journal of Education for Students Placed At Risk, 5*(1 & 2), 3–25.

Boykin, A. W., & Noguera, P. (2011). *Creating the opportunity to learning: Moving from research to practice to close the achievement gap.* Alexandria, VA: ASCD.

Boykin, A. W., Tyler, K. M., & Miller, O. A. (2005). In search of cultural themes and their expressions in the dynamics of classroom life. *Urban Education, 40,* 521–49.

Brafman, O., & Brafman, R. (2011). *Click: The magic of instant connections.* New York: Crown Publishers.

Bransford, J. D., Brown, A. L., & Cocking, R. R. (Eds.). (2000). How people learn: Brain, mind, experience, and school (Expanded ed.). Washington, DC: National Academy Press.

Brookfield, S. (2000). *The skillful teacher.* New York: Jossey-Bass.

Brown, A. L., & Campione, J. C. (1994). Guided discovery in a community of learners. In K. McGilly (Ed.), *Classroom lessons: Integrating cognitive theory and classroom practice* (pp. 229–272). Cambridge, MA: MIT Press.

Bruckheimer, J. (Producer), Simpson, D. C. (Producer), & Smith, J. N. (Director). (1995). *Dangerous minds* [Motion picture]. United States: Warner Brothers.

Bryk, A. S., & Schneider, B. (2002). *Trust in schools: A core resource for improvement.* New York: Russell Sage Foundation.

Cabrera, D., & Colosi, L. (2012). *Thinking at every desk: Four simple skills to transform your classroom.* New York: W. Norton & Norton.

Caine, R., Caine, G., & Crowell, S. (1999). *Mindshifts: A brain-compatible process for professional development and the renewal of education.* Chicago, IL: Chicago Review Press.

Cammarota, J., & Romero, A. (2006). Critically compassionate intellectualism for Latina/o students: Raising voices above the silencing in our schools. *Multicultural Education, 14*(2), 16–23.

Carrion, V., Weems, C. F., & Reiss, A. (2007). Stress predicts brain changes in children: A pilot longitudinal study on youth stress, posttraumatic stress disorder, and the hippocampus. *Pediatrics, 119*(3).

Cazden, C. (2001). *Classroom discourse: The language of teaching and learning.* Portsmouth, NH: Heinemann.

Christensen, L. (2000). *Reading, writing, and rising up: Teaching about social justice and the power of the written word.* Milwaukee, WI: Rethinking Schools.

Christensen, L. (2009). *Teaching for joy and justice: Re-imagining the language arts classroom.* Milwaukee, WI: Rethinking Schools.

Cisneros, S. (1995). Only daughter. In L. Castillo-Speed (Ed.), *Latina: Women's voices from the borderlands.* New York: Touchstone/Simon & Schuster.

Cohen, G. L., & Steele, C. M. (2002). A barrier of mistrust: How stereotypes affect cross-race mentoring. In J. Aronson (Ed.), *Improving academic achievement: Impact of psychological factors on education* (pp. 305–331). Oxford, England: Academic Press.

Cohen, G. L., Steele, C. M., & Ross, L. D. (1999). The mentor's dilemma: Providing critical feedback across the racial divide. *Personality and Social Psychology Bulletin, 25,* 1302–1318.

Collins, J. (1988). Language and class in minority education. *Anthropology and Education Quarterly, 19*(4), 299–326.

Comer, J. (1997). *Waiting for a miracle: Why our schools can't solve our problems—and how we can.* New York: Dutton.

Covington, M. (1998). *The will to learn: A guide for motivating young people.* Cambridge, MA: Cambridge University Press.

Coyle, D. (2009). *The talent code: Greatness isn't born. It's grown. Here's how.* New York: Bantam.

Crocker, J., & Major, B. (1989). Social stigma and self-esteem: The self-protective properties of stigma. *Psychological Review, 96,* 608–630.

Cushman, K. (2005). *Fires in the bathroom: Advice for teachers from high school students.* New York: New Press.

Cushman, K. (2010). *Fires in the mind: What kids can tell us about motivation & mastery.* New York: Jossey-Bass.

Darling-Hammond, L. (2001). *The right to learn: A blueprint for creating schools that work.* San Francisco: Jossey-Bass.

Darling-Hammond, L. (2010). *The flat world and education: How America's commitment to equity will determine our future.* New York: Teachers College Press.

Dean, J. (2006). The future of driving. *Rethinking Schools, 21*(2).

Delpit, L. (1988). The silenced dialogue: Power and pedagogy in educating other people's children. *Harvard Educational Review, 58*(3), 280–298.

Delpit, L. (1995). *Other people's children: Cultural conflict in the classroom.* New York: New Press.

Delpit, L., & Dowdy, J. K. (Eds.). (2002). *The skin that we speak: Thoughts on language and culture in the classroom.* New York: New Press.

Dray, B., & Wisneski, D. (2011). Mindful reflection as a process for developing culturally responsive practices. *TEACHING Exceptional Children, 44*(1), 28–36.

Dunbar, P. L. (1997). *Selected poems.* Mineola, NY: Dover.

Duncan-Andrade, J. (2007). Gangstas, wankstas, and ridas: Defining, developing, and supporting effective teachers in urban schools. *International Journal of Qualitative Studies in Education, 20*(6), 617–638.

Duncan-Andrade, J. (2009). Note to educators: Hope required when growing roses in concrete. *Harvard Education Review, 79*(2), 181–194.

Dweck, C. (2007). *Mindset: The new psychology of success.* New York: Ballantine Books.

Education Trust. (2006). *Teaching inequality: How poor and minority students are shortchanged on teacher quality.* Washington, DC: The Education Trust.

Farrington, C. A., Roderick, M., Allensworth, E., Nagaoka, J., Keyes, T. S., Johnson, D. W., & Beechum, N. O. (2012). *Teaching adolescents to become learners: The role of noncognitive factors in shaping school performance: A critical literature review.* Chicago: University of Chicago Consortium on Chicago School Research.

Ford, D. Y., Moore, J. L., III, & Whiting, G. W. (2006). Eliminating deficit orientations: Creating classrooms and curriculums for gifted students from diverse cultural backgrounds. In M. G. Constantine & D. W. Sue (Eds.), *Addressing racism: Facilitating cultural competence in mental health and educational settings* (pp. 173–193). Hoboken, NJ: Wiley.

Freire, P. (1993). *Pedagogy of the oppressed.* New York: Continuum.

Freire, P. (1997). *Pedagogy of hope.* New York: Continuum.

Fullan, M. (2007). *Leading in a culture of change.* San Francisco: Jossey-Bass.

Gay, G. (2010). *Culturally responsive teaching: Theory, research, and practice.* New York: Teachers College Press.

Gee, J. P. (2004). *Situated language and learning: A critique of traditional schooling.* New York: Routledge.

Giovanni, N. (1993). *Ego trippin' and other poems for young people.* Chicago: Chicago Review Press.

Gopnik, A., Meltzoff, A., & Kuhl, P. (2000). *The scientist in the crib: What early learning tells us about the mind.* New York: William Morrow.

Gordon, E. W. (1999). *Education and justice: A view from the back of the bus.* New York: Teachers College Press.

Gordon, E. W. (2001). The affirmative development of academic abilities. *Pedagogical Inquiry and Praxis, 1*(1), 1–4.

Gorski, P. (2008). The myth of the culture of poverty. *Education Leadership, 65*(7), 32–36.

Gudykunst, W. B., & Kim, Y. Y. (2003). *Communicating with strangers* (2nd ed.). Boston: McGraw-Hill.

Gutierrez, K. (2008). Developing a sociocritical literacy in the third space. *Reading Research Quarterly, 43*(2), 148–164.

Haberman, M. (1991, December). The pedagogy of poverty versus good teaching. *Phi Delta Kappan, 73*(4), 290–294

Hanson, R. (2013). *Hardwiring happiness: The new brain science of contentment, calm, and confidence.* New York, NY: Harmony Books.

Hasson, U., Ghazanfar, A. A., Galantucci, B., Garrod, S., & Keysers, C. (2010). Brain-to-brain coupling: Mechanism for creating and sharing a social world. *Trends in Cognitive Science, 16*(2), 114–121.

Hattie, J., & Timperley, H. (2007, March). The power of feedback. *Review of Educational Research, 77*(1), 81–112.

Heath, C., & Heath, D. (2007). *Made to stick: Why some ideas survive and others die.* New York: Random House.

Hernandez-Sheets, R. (2009). What is diversity pedagogy? *Multicultural Education, 16*(3), 11–17.

Hilliard, A., III. (1989). Teachers and cultural styles in a pluralistic society. *NEA Today, 7*(6), 65–69.

Hilliard, A., III. (1995). *The maroon within us: Selected essays on African American community socialization.* New York: Black Classic Press.

Hofstede, G. (2001). *Culture's consequences: Comparing values, behaviors, institutions and organizations across nations.* Thousand Oaks, CA: Sage.

Hofstede, G., Hofstede, G. J., & Minkov, M. (2010). *Cultures and organizations: Software of the mind.* New York: McGraw-Hill.

Holmes, R. M. (1995). *How young children perceive race.* Thousand Oaks, CA: Sage.

Holzgang, C. (Producer), Campion, C. (Producer), & Levin, P. (Director). (1981). *The Marva Collins story* [Television movie]. United States: Hallmark Hall of Fame.

hooks, b. (1994). *Teaching to transgress: Education as the practice of freedom.* New York: Routledge.

Howard, G. R. (2002). School improvement for all: Reflections on the achievement gap. *Journal of School Improvement, 3*(1), 9.

Hyerle, D. N. (1996). *Visual tools to construct knowledge.* Alexandria, VA: ASCD.

Hyerle, D. N., & Alper, L. (2011). *Student success with thinking maps* (2nd ed.). Thousand Oaks, CA: Corwin.

Irvine, J. J. (2003). *Educating teachers for diversity: Seeing with a cultural eye.* New York: Teachers College Press.

Jackson, Y. (2011). *The pedagogy of confidence: Inspiring high intellectual performance in urban schools.* New York: Teachers College Press.

Johnston, P. (2004). *Choice words: How our language affects children's learning.* Portland, ME: Stenhouse.

Johnston, P. (2012). *Opening minds: Using language to change lives.* Portland, ME: Stenhouse.

Kalyanpur, M., & Harry, B. (2012). *Cultural reciprocity in special education: Building family-professional relationships.* Baltimore: Paul H. Brookes.

Kirwan Institute for the Study of Race and Ethnicity. (2013). *Understanding implicit bias: The state of science.* Columbus, OH: Author.

Kleinfeld, J. (1972). *Effective teachers of Indian and Eskimo high school students.* Fairbanks: University of Alaska, Institute of Social, Economic, and Government Research.

Kleinfeld, J. (1975). Effective teachers of Eskimo and Indian students. *School Review, 83*(2), 301–344.

Knight, J. (2013). *High-impact instruction.* Thousand Oaks, CA: Corwin.

Kohli, R., & Solórzano, D. (2012). Teachers, please learn our names!: Racial microaggressions and the K–12 classroom. *Race, Ethnicity, and Education, 15*(4), 441–462.

Kozol, J. (2006). *The shame of the nation: The restoration of apartheid schooling in America.* New York: Broadway Books.

Ladson-Billings, G. (2009). *The dreamkeepers: Successful teachers of African-American children* (2nd ed.). San Francisco: Jossey-Bass.

Lemov, D. (2010). *Teach like a champion: 49 techniques that put students on the path to college.* San Francisco: Jossey-Bass.

Marshall, P. L. (2002). *Cultural diversity in our schools.* Belmont, CA: Wadsworth/ Thomson Learning.

Marzano, R. (2004). *Building background knowledge for academic achievement.* Alexandria, VA: ASCD.

McDonald, J., Mohr, N., Dichter, A., & McDonald, E. (2013). *The power of protocols: An educator's guide to better practice* (3rd ed.). New York: Teachers College Press.

McIntosh, P. (1990). White privilege: Unpacking the invisible knapsack. *Independent School, 90*(49), 31–35.

Means, B., & Knapp, M. S. (1991). Rethinking teaching for disadvantaged students. In B. Means, C. Chelemer, & M. S. Knapp (Eds.), *Teaching advanced skills to at-risk students: Views from research and practice* (pp. 1–26). San Francisco: Jossey-Bass.

Medina, J. J. (2008). *Brain rules: 12 Principles for surviving and thriving at work, home, and school.* Seattle, WA: Pear Press.

Merzenich, M. (2013). *Soft-wired: How the new science of brain plasticity can change your life.* San Francisco: Parnassus Publishing.

Moll, L., Gonzales, N., & Amanti, C. (2005). *Funds of knowledge: Theorizing practices in households, communities, and classrooms.* New Jersey: Lawrence Erlbaum Associates.

Moses, R., & Cobb, C. (2002). *Radical equations: Civil Rights from Mississippi to the Algebra Project.* Boston: Beacon Press.

Musca, T. (Producer), & Menendez, R. (Director). (1988). *Stand and deliver* [Motion picture]. United States: Warner Brothers.

National Research Council. (2000). *How people learn: Brain, mind, experience and school.* Washington, DC: National Academy Press.

National Study Group for the Affirmative Development of Academic Ability. (2004). *All students reaching the top: Strategies for closing academic achievement gaps.* Naperville, IL: Learning Point Associates.

Nieto, S. (2009). *The light in their eyes: Creating multicultural learning communities* (10th Anniversary Ed.). New York: Teachers College Press.

Nieto, S., & Bode, P. (2007). *Affirming diversity: The sociopolitical context of multicultural education.* Boston: Allyn & Bacon.

Noddings, N. (1992). *The challenge to care in schools: An alternative approach to education.* New York: Teachers College Press.

Oakes, J. (2005). *Keeping track: How schools structure inequality.* New Haven, CT: Yale University Press.

Obidah, J., & Teel, K. (2001). *Because of the kids: Facing racial and cultural differences in schools.* New York: Teachers College Press.

Offermann, L., & Rosh, L. (2012). Building trust through skillful self-disclosure. *Harvard Business Review Blog.* Retrieved from http://blogs.hbr.org/2012/06/instantaneous-intimacy-skillfu/

Payne, C. (2008). *So much reform, so little change: The persistence of failure in urban schools.* Cambridge, MA: Harvard Education Press.

Pink, D. (2011). *Drive: The surprising truth about what motivates us.* New York: Riverhead Books.

Pollack, M. (2005). *Colormute: Race talk dilemmas in an American school.* Princeton, NJ: Princeton University Press.

Pollack, M. (2008). *Everyday anti-racism: Getting real about race in school.* New York: New Press.

Porges, S. (2011). *The polyvagal theory: Neurophysiological foundations of emotions, attachment, communication, and self-regulation.* New York: W. W. Norton & Company.

Quiroz, P. A. (1997). *The "silencing" of the lambs: How Latino students lose their "voice" in school* (ISRI Working Paper No. 31). East Lansing: Michigan State University, Julian Samora Research Institute.

Quiroz, P. A. (2001). The silencing of the Latino student "voice": Puerto Rican and Mexican narratives in eighth grade and high school. *Anthropology & Education Quarterly, 32*(3), 326–349.

Resnick, L. (1987). *Education and learning to think.* Washington, DC: National Academy Press.

Rigney, D. (2010). *The Matthew effect: How advantage begets further advantage.* New York: Columbia University Press.

Ritchhart, R. (2002). *Intellectual character: What it is, why it matters, and how to get it.* San Francisco: Jossey-Bass.

Ritchhart, R., Church, M., & Morrison, K. (2011). *Making thinking visible: How to promote engagement, understanding and independence for all learners.* San Francisco: Jossey-Bass.

Rock, D. (2009). Managing with the brain in mind. *Oxford Leadership Journal, 1*(1), 1–10.

Seligman, M. (2006). *Learned optimism: How to change your mind and your life.* New York: Vintage.

Simon, T. (Producer). (2009, December 6). The Zone: Geoffery Canada and the Harlem Children's Zone [Program segment]. *60 Minutes* [Television broadcast]. New York: CBS.

Skiba, R. J., Peterson, R. L., & Williams, T. (1997). Office referrals and suspension: Disciplinary intervention in middle schools. *Education and Treatment of Children, 20,* 295–315.

Skiba, R., & Sprague, J. (2008). Safety without suspensions. *Educational Leadership, 66*(1), 38–43.

Small, M. (1998). *Our babies, ourselves: How biology and culture shape the parents we become.* New York: Anchor.

Snipes, J., Fancsali, C., & Stoker, G. (2012). *Student academic mindset interventions: A review of the current landscape.* San Francisco: The Stupski Foundation.

Solórzano, D. G., & Yosso, T. J. (2001). From racial stereotyping and deficit discourse toward a critical race theory in teacher education. *Multicultural Education, 9*(1), 2–8.

Sousa, D. (2001). *How the brain learns.* Thousand Oaks: Corwin.

Spindler, G., & Spindler, L. (1982). Roger Harker and Schonhausen: From familiar to strange and back again. In G. Spindler (Ed.), *Doing the ethnography of schooling: Educational anthropology in action* (pp. 21–43). Prospect Heights, IL: Waveland Press, Inc.

Steele, C. M. (1992). Race and the schooling of black Americans. *The Atlantic Monthly, 269*(4), 68–78.

Steele, C. M. (1999). "Stereotype threat" and black college students. *The Atlantic Monthly, 284*(2), 44–54.

Steele, C. (2011). *Whistling Vivaldi: How stereotypes affect us and what we can do.* New York: W.W. Norton & Co.

Sternberg, R. J. (2002). Raising the achievement of all students: Teaching for successful intelligence. *Educational Psychology Review, 14*(4), 383–393.

Stiggins, R., Arter, J., Chappuis, J., & Chappuis, S. (2004). *Classroom assessment for student learning: Doing it right—using it well.* Portland, OR: ETS Assessment Training Institute.

Sue, D., Capodilupo, C., Torino, G., Bucceri, J., Holder, A., Nadal, K., & Esquilin, M. (2007). Racial microaggressions in everyday life: Implications for clinical practice. *American Psychologist, 62*(4), 271–286.

Sylwester, R. (1995). *A celebration of neurons: An educator's guide to the human brain.* Alexandria, VA: ASCD.

Tatum, A. (2009). *Reading for their life: (Re) Building the textual lineages of African American adolescent males.* Portsmouth, NH: Heinemann.

Tharp, R., & Gallimore, R. (1991). *The instructional conversation: Teaching and learning in social activity* (Research Report 2). Berkeley, CA: Center for Research on Education, Diversity, and Excellence.

Tough, P. (2013). *How children succeed: Grit, curiosity, and the hidden power of character.* Boston: Mariner Books.

Trumbull, E., Rothstein-Fisch, C., Greenfield, P., & Quiroz, P. (2001). *Bridging cultures between home and school: A guide for teachers.* San Francisco: WestEd.

Valdes, G. (1996). *Con respeto: Bridging the distances between culturally diverse families and schools.* New York: Teachers College Press.

Van Ausdale, D., & Feagin, J. R. (2001). *The first R: How children learn race and racism.* Lanham, MD: Rowman & Littlefield.

Villegas, A., & Lucas, T. (2002). Preparing culturally responsive teachers rethinking the curriculum. *Journal of Teacher Education, 53*(1), 20–32.

Vygotsky, L. S. (1978). *Mind in society: The development of higher psychological processes.* Cambridge, MA: Harvard University Press.

Ware, F. (2006). Warm demander pedagogy: Culturally responsive teaching that supports a culture of achievement for African American students. *Urban Education, 41*(4), 427–456.

Washburn, K. (2010). *The architecture of learning: Designing instruction for the learning brain.* Pelham, AL: Clerestory Press.

Wheeler, R., & Swords, R. (2006). *Code-switching: Teaching standard English in urban classrooms.* Urbana, IL: National Council of Teachers of English.

Wiliam, D. (2004). *Assessment and the regulation of learning.* Paper presented at the annual meeting of the National Council on Measurement in Education, San Diego, CA. Retrieved from http://www.dylanwiliam.org/Dylan_Wiliams_website/Papers_files/NCME%2004%20paper.pdf

Willingham, D. T. (2003). Students remember what they think about. *American Educator, 27*(2), 37–41.

Willis, J. (2006). *Research-based strategies to ignite student learning: Insights from a neurologist/classroom teacher.* Alexandria, VA: ASCD.

Wise, T. (2011). *White like me: Reflections on race from a privileged son.* Berkeley: Soft Skull Press.

Wormeli, R. (2009). *Metaphors & analogies: Power tools for teaching any subject.* Portland, ME: Stenhouse.

Zull, J. E. (2002). *The art of the changing brain: Enriching the practice of teaching by exploring the biology of learning.* Sterling, VA: Stylus Publishing.

Zwiers, J., & Crawford, M. (2011). *Academic conversations: Classroom talk that fosters critical thinking and content understandings.* Portland, ME: Stenhouse.

Index

A SAGE Company

Corwin is committed to improving education for all learners by publishing books and other professional development resources for those serving the field of PreK–12 education. By providing practical, hands-on materials, Corwin continues to carry out the promise of its motto: **"Helping Educators Do Their Work Better."**